American Spirit

Student Workbook | Part 1

Building Confidence

A Demme Learning Publication

American Spirit Student Workbook, Parts 1 and 2
©2014 Spelling You See
©2013 Karen J. Holinga, PhD
Published and distributed by Demme Learning

spellingyousee.com

1-888-854-6284 or +1 717-283-1448 | demmelearning.com
Lancaster, Pennsylvania USA

ISBN 978-1-60826-615-9 (American Spirit Student Workbook)
ISBN 978-1-60826-616-6 (Part 1)

Printed in the United States of America
Revision Code 1118-C

Printed in the United States of America by Innovative Technologies in Print

For information regarding CPSIA on this printed material call: 1-888-854-6284
and provide reference #1118-11022020

To the Instructor

This innovative program is designed to help your student become a confident and successful speller while spending only a few minutes each day on spelling practice. The program is not difficult, but it is different. Your *Instructor's Handbook* is essential in order to teach this program effectively.

Before you begin, take time to read **Getting Started** in the *Handbook*, as well as the detailed directions for the first few lessons. As you move through the various activities, you will also want to read more details about each one in the **Weekly Activity Guide**. There is an answer key in the back of the *Handbook* that shows exactly how each passage in the student book should be marked.

For a more in-depth understanding of the program, read the sections about the philosophy and the developmental stages of spelling. You will also find the answers to **Frequently Asked Questions** helpful.

1. Read the story to your student.

2. Read it together slowly. Encourage your student to look carefully at each word.

3. Vowel chunks are a combination of vowels that usually make one sound. Help your student find and mark all the **vowel chunks** in yellow.

Colonial children liked having fun as much as you do. Of course, they didn't have video games or movies. They found many other ways to have a good time. They played tag, hopscotch, and hide and seek. They rolled hoops, shot marbles, and beat drums. They played with dolls and tea sets. A group could play rounders, a game something like baseball. Colonial children worked hard. They also found many ways to play.

Vowel Chunks

aa ae ai ao au aw ay

ea ee ei eo ew ey eau

ia ie ii io iu

oa oe oi oo ou ow oy

ua ue ui uo uy

Copy the story and mark the vowel chunks that you marked in Section 1.

Colonial children liked having fun

Colonial children liked having fun

as much as you do. Of course,

as much as you do. Of course,

they didn't have video games or

they didn't have video games or

movies. They found many other

movies. They found many other

ways to have a good time. They

ways to have a good time. They

played tag, hopscotch, and hide

played tag, hopscotch, and hide

and seek. They rolled hoops, shot

and seek. They rolled hoops, shot

marbles, and beat drums. They

marbles, and beat drums. They

played with dolls and tea sets.

played with dolls and tea sets.

1. Read the story to your student.

2. Read it together slowly. Encourage your student to look carefully at each word.

3. Work with your student to find all the <u>**vowel chunks**</u> and mark them in yellow.

Colonial children liked having fun as much as you do. Of course, they didn't have video games or movies. They found many other ways to have a good time. They played tag, hopscotch, and hide and seek. They rolled hoops, shot marbles, and beat drums. They played with dolls and tea sets. A group could play rounders, a game something like baseball. Colonial children worked hard. They also found many ways to play.

Vowel Chunks

aa ae ai ao au aw ay

ea ee ei eo ew ey eau

ia ie ii io iu

oa oe oi oo ou ow oy

ua ue ui uo uy

Section 2: Copywork

Copy and "chunk" the story. Look at the opposite page if you need help.

They played tag, hopscotch, and

They played tag, hopscotch, and

hide and seek. They rolled hoops,

hide and seek. They rolled hoops,

shot marbles, and beat drums.

shot marbles, and beat drums.

They played with dolls and tea

They played with dolls and tea

sets. A group could play rounders,

sets. A group could play rounders,

a game something like baseball.

a game something like baseball.

Colonial children worked hard.

Colonial children worked hard.

They also found many ways

They also found many ways

to play.

to play.

1. Read the story to your student.

2. Read it together slowly. Encourage your student to look carefully at each word.

3. Together, find all the <u>vowel chunks</u> in the passage and mark them in yellow.

Colonial children liked having fun as much as you do. Of course, they didn't have video games or movies. They found many other ways to have a good time. They played tag, hopscotch, and hide and seek. They rolled hoops, shot marbles, and beat drums. They played with dolls and tea sets. A group could play rounders, a game something like baseball. Colonial children worked hard. They also found many ways to play.

Vowel Chunks

aa	ae	ai	ao	au	aw	ay
ea	ee	ei	eo	ew	ey	eau
ia	ie	ii	io	iu		
oa	oe	oi	oo	ou	ow	oy
ua	ue	ui	uo	uy		

Copy and chunk the story. Look at the opposite page if you need help.

Colonial children liked having fun

Colonial children liked having fun

as much as you do. Of course,

as much as you do. Of course,

they didn't have video games or

they didn't have video games or

movies. They found many other

movies. They found many other

ways to have a good time. They

ways to have a good time. They

played tag, hopscotch, and hide

played tag, hopscotch, and hide

and seek. They rolled hoops, shot

and seek. They rolled hoops, shot

marbles, and beat drums. They

marbles, and beat drums. They

played with dolls and tea sets.

played with dolls and tea sets.

1. Read the story to your student.

2. Read it together slowly. Encourage your student to look carefully at each word.

3. Together, find all the **vowel chunks** in the passage and mark them in yellow.

4. Before doing the dictation, be sure to watch the video demonstrating how to do it. All the passages in this workbook are also in the *Instructor's Handbook* under Resources. When dictating the passage, you may want to cover this page with a piece of paper and read the story from the *Handbook*.

Colonial children liked having fun as much as you do. Of course, they didn't have video games or movies. They found many other ways to have a good time. They played tag, hopscotch, and hide and seek. They rolled hoops, shot marbles, and beat drums. They played with dolls and tea sets. A group could play rounders, a game something like baseball. Colonial children worked hard. They also found many ways to play.

Vowel Chunks

aa	ae	ai	ao	au	aw	ay
ea	ee	ei	eo	ew	ey	eau
ia	ie	ii	io	iu		
oa	oe	oi	oo	ou	ow	oy
ua	ue	ui	uo	uy		

Section 2: First Dictation

Write this week's story from dictation. Take your time and ask for help if you need it.

Colonial

I spelled _____ words correctly.

1. Read the story to your student.

2. Read it together slowly. Encourage your student to look carefully at each word.

3. Together, find all the <u>**vowel chunks**</u> in the passage and mark them in yellow.

Colonial children liked having fun as much as you do. Of course, they didn't have video games or movies. They found many other ways to have a good time. They played tag, hopscotch, and hide and seek. They rolled hoops, shot marbles, and beat drums. They played with dolls and tea sets. A group could play rounders, a game something like baseball. Colonial children worked hard. They also found many ways to play.

Vowel Chunks

aa	ae	ai	ao	au	aw	ay
ea	ee	ei	eo	ew	ey	eau
ia	ie	ii	io	iu		
oa	oe	oi	oo	ou	ow	oy
ua	ue	ui	uo	uy		

Section 2: Second Dictation

See if you can write this week's story from dictation without asking for help.

I spelled _____ words correctly.

1. Read the story to your student.

2. Read it together slowly. Encourage your student to look carefully at each word.

3. Together, find all the <u>**vowel chunks**</u> in the passage and mark them in yellow.

A frail little slave girl was sold to the Wheatley family. They named her Phillis after the slave ship that had brought her to Boston. Slaves were not allowed to go to school. The Wheatleys taught Phillis to read and write. She learned very quickly. As a teenager, Phillis Wheatley began writing poems. She was the first African American poet to have her poems printed.

Vowel Chunks

aa	ae	ai	ao	au	aw	ay
ea	ee	ei	eo	ew	ey	eau
ia	ie	ii	io	iu		
oa	oe	oi	oo	ou	ow	oy
ua	ue	ui	uo	uy		

Copy and chunk the story. Look at the opposite page if you need help.

A frail little slave girl was sold

A

to the Wheatley family. They

t

named her Phillis after the slave

n

ship that had brought her to

s

Boston. Slaves were not allowed

B

to go to school. The Wheatleys

t

taught Phillis to read and write.

t

She learned very quickly.

S

1. Read the story to your student.

2. Read it together slowly. Encourage your student to look carefully at each word.

3. Together, find all the <u>vowel chunks</u> in the passage and mark them in yellow.

A frail little slave girl was sold to the Wheatley family. They named her Phillis after the slave ship that had brought her to Boston. Slaves were not allowed to go to school. The Wheatleys taught Phillis to read and write. She learned very quickly. As a teenager, Phillis Wheatley began writing poems. She was the first African American poet to have her poems printed.

Vowel Chunks

aa ae ai ao au aw ay

ea ee ei eo ew ey eau

ia ie ii io iu

oa oe oi oo ou ow oy

ua ue ui uo uy

Section 2: Copywork

Copy and chunk the story. Look at the opposite page if you need help.

Slaves were not allowed to

S

go to school. The Wheatleys

g

taught Phillis to read and write.

t

She learned very quickly. As a

S

teenager, Phillis Wheatley began

t

writing poems. She was the first

w

African American poet to have

A

her poems printed.

h

1. Read the story to your student.

2. Read it together slowly. Encourage your student to look carefully at each word.

3. Together, find all the **vowel chunks** in the passage and mark them in yellow.

A frail little slave girl was sold to the Wheatley family. They named her Phillis after the slave ship that had brought her to Boston. Slaves were not allowed to go to school. The Wheatleys taught Phillis to read and write. She learned very quickly. As a teenager, Phillis Wheatley began writing poems. She was the first African American poet to have her poems printed.

Vowel Chunks

aa	ae	ai	ao	au	aw	ay
ea	ee	ei	eo	ew	ey	eau
ia	ie	ii	io	iu		
oa	oe	oi	oo	ou	ow	oy
ua	ue	ui	uo	uy		

Copy and chunk the story. Look at the opposite page if you need help.

A frail little slave girl was sold

A

to the Wheatley family. They

t

named her Phillis after the slave

n

ship that had brought her to

s

Boston. Slaves were not allowed

B

to go to school. The Wheatleys

t

taught Phillis to read and write.

t

She learned very quickly.

S

1. Read the story to your student.

2. Read it together slowly. Encourage your student to look carefully at each word.

3. Together, find all the **vowel chunks** in the passage and mark them in yellow.

A frail little slave girl was sold to the Wheatley family. They named her Phillis after the slave ship that had brought her to Boston. Slaves were not allowed to go to school. The Wheatleys taught Phillis to read and write. She learned very quickly. As a teenager, Phillis Wheatley began writing poems. She was the first African American poet to have her poems printed.

Vowel Chunks

aa	ae	ai	ao	au	aw	ay
ea	ee	ei	eo	ew	ey	eau
ia	ie	ii	io	iu		
oa	oe	oi	oo	ou	ow	oy
ua	ue	ui	uo	uy		

Section 2: First Dictation

Write this week's story from dictation. Take your time and ask for help if you need it.

A

I spelled _____ words correctly.

1. Read the story to your student.

2. Read it together slowly. Encourage your student to look carefully at each word.

3. Together, find all the **vowel chunks** in the passage and mark them in yellow.

A frail little slave girl was sold to the Wheatley family. They named her Phillis after the slave ship that had brought her to Boston. Slaves were not allowed to go to school. The Wheatleys taught Phillis to read and write. She learned very quickly. As a teenager, Phillis Wheatley began writing poems. She was the first African American poet to have her poems printed.

Vowel Chunks

aa	ae	ai	ao	au	aw	ay
ea	ee	ei	eo	ew	ey	eau
ia	ie	ii	io	iu		
oa	oe	oi	oo	ou	ow	oy
ua	ue	ui	uo	uy		

Section 2: Second Dictation

See if you can write this week's story from dictation without asking for help.

I spelled _____ words correctly.

1. Read the story to your student.

2. Read it together slowly. Have the student look carefully at each word as you read.

3. Help your student look for and mark all the **consonant chunks** in blue.

Benjamin Franklin loved swimming. He wanted to swim even faster. He shaped two pieces of thin wood into ovals. He cut a hole in each for his thumb. He may have gotten the idea from amphibians like frogs that have webbed feet. Ben swam much faster with these wooden fins, but he stopped using them. They made his wrists tired. Franklin had many other great ideas!

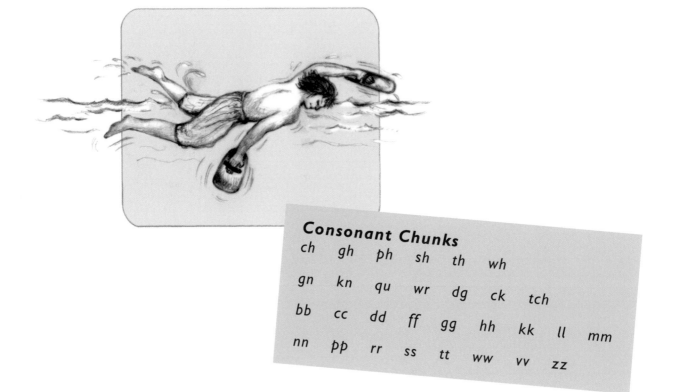

Consonant Chunks

ch gh ph sh th wh

gn kn qu wr dg ck tch

bb cc dd ff gg hh kk ll mm

nn pp rr ss tt ww vv zz

Copy and chunk the story. Look at the opposite page if you need help.

Benjamin Franklin loved

B

swimming. He wanted to swim

s

even faster. He shaped two

e

pieces of thin wood into ovals.

P

He cut a hole in each for

H

his thumb. He may have gotten

h

the idea from amphibians like

t

frogs that have webbed feet.

f

Ben swam much faster

B

1. Read the story to your student.

2. Read it together slowly. Have the student look carefully at each word as you read.

3. Help your student look for and mark all the <u>**consonant chunks**</u> in blue. Notice that a consonant chunk may have a different sound than the individual letters do.

Benjamin Franklin loved swimming. He wanted to swim even faster. He shaped two pieces of thin wood into ovals. He cut a hole in each for his thumb. He may have gotten the idea from amphibians like frogs that have webbed feet. Ben swam much faster with these wooden fins, but he stopped using them. They made his wrists tired. Franklin had many other great ideas!

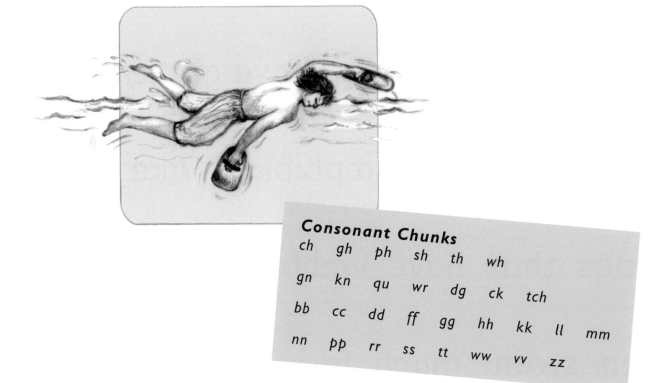

Consonant Chunks

ch	gh	ph	sh	th	wh			
gn	kn	qu	wr	dg	ck	tch		
bb	cc	dd	ff	gg	hh	kk	ll	mm
nn	pp	rr	ss	tt	ww	vv	zz	

Copy and chunk the story. Look at the opposite page if you need help.

He cut a hole in each for

H

his thumb. He may have gotten

h

the idea from amphibians like

t

frogs that have webbed feet.

f

Ben swam much faster with

B

these wooden fins, but he

t

stopped using them. They made

s

his wrists tired. Franklin had

h

many other great ideas!

m

1. Read the story to your student.

2. Read it together slowly. Have the student look carefully at each word as you read.

3. Help your student look for and mark all the <u>**consonant chunks**</u> in blue.

Benjamin Franklin loved swimming. He wanted to swim even faster. He shaped two pieces of thin wood into ovals. He cut a hole in each for his thumb. He may have gotten the idea from amphibians like frogs that have webbed feet. Ben swam much faster with these wooden fins, but he stopped using them. They made his wrists tired. Franklin had many other great ideas!

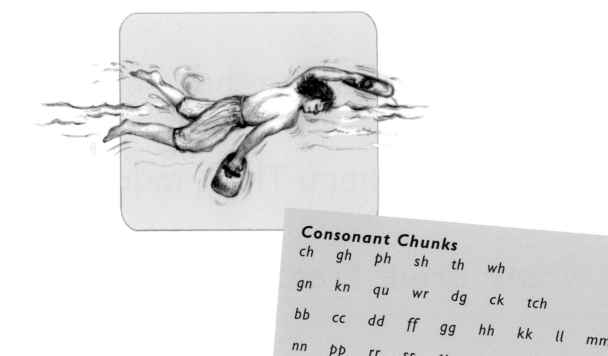

Consonant Chunks

ch	gh	ph	sh	th	wh			
gn	kn	qu	wr	dg	ck	tch		
bb	cc	dd	ff	gg	hh	kk	ll	mm
nn	pp	rr	ss	tt	ww	vv	zz	

Copy and chunk the story. Look at the opposite page if you need help.

Benjamin Franklin loved

B

swimming. He wanted to swim

s

even faster. He shaped two

e

pieces of thin wood into ovals.

P

He cut a hole in each for

H

his thumb. He may have gotten

h

the idea from amphibians like

t

frogs that have webbed feet.

f

Ben swam much faster

B

1. Read the story to your student.

2. Read it together slowly. Have the student look carefully at each word as you read.

3. Together, find all the <u>**consonant chunks**</u> in the passage and mark them in blue.

Benjamin Franklin loved swimming. He wanted to swim even faster. He shaped two pieces of thin wood into ovals. He cut a hole in each for his thumb. He may have gotten the idea from amphibians like frogs that have webbed feet. Ben swam much faster with these wooden fins, but he stopped using them. They made his wrists tired. Franklin had many other great ideas!

Consonant Chunks

ch	gh	ph	sh	th	wh		
gn	kn	qu	wr	dg	ck	tch	
bb	cc	dd	ff	gg	hh	kk	ll	mm
nn	pp	rr	ss	tt	ww	vv	zz

Section 2: First Dictation

Write this week's story from dictation. Take your time and ask for help if you need it.

Benjamin

I spelled _____ words correctly.

1. Read the story to your student.

2. Read it together slowly. Have the student look carefully at each word as you read.

3. Together, find all the <u>**consonant chunks**</u> in the passage and mark them in blue.

Benjamin Franklin loved swimming. He wanted to swim even faster. He shaped two pieces of thin wood into ovals. He cut a hole in each for his thumb. He may have gotten the idea from amphibians like frogs that have webbed feet. Ben swam much faster with these wooden fins, but he stopped using them. They made his wrists tired. Franklin had many other great ideas!

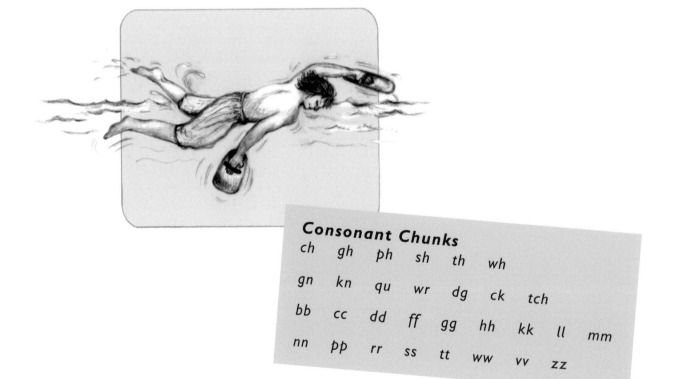

Consonant Chunks

ch	gh	ph	sh	th	wh
gn	kn	qu	wr	dg	ck	tch
bb	cc	dd	ff	gg	hh	kk	ll	mm
nn	pp	rr	ss	tt	ww	vv	zz

Section 2: Second Dictation

See if you can write this week's story from dictation without asking for help.

I spelled _____ words correctly.

1. Read the story to your student.

2. Read it together slowly. Have the student look carefully at each word as you read.

3. Help your student look for and mark all the **consonant chunks** in blue.

In colonial times, people used quill pens to write. A quill is the hollow shaft inside a feather. The tip of the feather is cut to form a point. Then the shaft is filled with ink. Learning to write with a quill pen takes time and practice. After every few words, the pen runs out of ink. Then you must refill it from an inkwell. The ballpoint pens we have today are much easier to use!

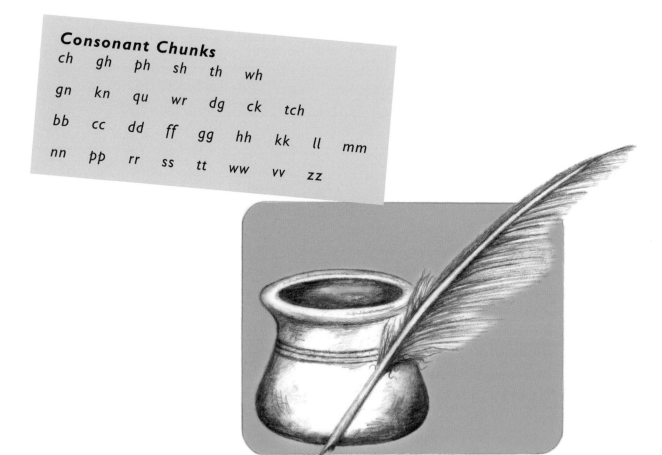

Consonant Chunks

ch gh ph sh th wh

gn kn qu wr dg ck tch

bb cc dd ff gg hh kk ll mm

nn pp rr ss tt ww vv zz

Copy and chunk the story. Look at the opposite page if you need help.

In colonial times, people used

quill pens to write. A quill is the

hollow shaft inside a feather.

The tip of the feather is cut to

form a point. Then the shaft is

filled with ink. Learning to write

with a quill pen takes time and

practice. After every few words,

the pen runs out of ink.

1. Read the story to your student.

2. Read it together slowly. Have the student look carefully at each word as you read.

3. Help your student look for and mark all the **consonant chunks** in blue.

In colonial times, people used quill pens to write. A quill is the hollow shaft inside a feather. The tip of the feather is cut to form a point. Then the shaft is filled with ink. Learning to write with a quill pen takes time and practice. After every few words, the pen runs out of ink. Then you must refill it from an inkwell. The ballpoint pens we have today are much easier to use!

Consonant Chunks

ch   gh   ph   sh   th   wh

gn   kn   qu   wr   dg   ck   tch

bb   cc   dd   ff   gg   hh   kk   ll   mm

nn   pp   rr   ss   tt   ww   vv   zz

Copy and chunk the story. Look at the opposite page if you need help.

The tip of the feather is cut to

T

form a point. Then the shaft is

f

filled with ink. Learning to write

f

with a quill pen takes time and

w

practice. After every few words,

p

the pen runs out of ink. Then

t

you must refill it from an inkwell.

y

The ballpoint pens we have today

T

are much easier to use!

a

1. Read the story to your student.

2. Read it together slowly. Have the student look carefully at each word as you read.

3. Help your student look for and mark all the **consonant chunks** in blue.

In colonial times, people used quill pens to write. A quill is the hollow shaft inside a feather. The tip of the feather is cut to form a point. Then the shaft is filled with ink. Learning to write with a quill pen takes time and practice. After every few words, the pen runs out of ink. Then you must refill it from an inkwell. The ballpoint pens we have today are much easier to use!

Consonant Chunks

ch   gh   ph   sh   th   wh

gn   kn   qu   wr   dg   ck   tch

bb   cc   dd   ff   gg   hh   kk   ll   mm

nn   pp   rr   ss   tt   ww   vv   zz

Copy and chunk the story. Look at the opposite page if you need help.

In colonial times, people used

l

quill pens to write. A quill is the

q

hollow shaft inside a feather.

h

The tip of the feather is cut to

T

form a point. Then the shaft is

f

filled with ink. Learning to write

f

with a quill pen takes time and

w

practice. After every few words,

p

the pen runs out of ink.

t

1. Read the story to your student.

2. Read it together slowly. Have the student look carefully at each word as you read.

3. Together, find all the **consonant chunks** in the passage and mark them in blue.

In colonial times, people used quill pens to write. A quill is the hollow shaft inside a feather. The tip of the feather is cut to form a point. Then the shaft is filled with ink. Learning to write with a quill pen takes time and practice. After every few words, the pen runs out of ink. Then you must refill it from an inkwell. The ballpoint pens we have today are much easier to use!

Consonant Chunks

ch	gh	ph	sh	th	wh
gn	kn	qu	wr	dg	ck	tch
bb	cc	dd	ff	gg	hh	kk	ll	mm
nn	pp	rr	ss	tt	ww	vv	zz

Section 2: First Dictation

Write this week's story from dictation. Take your time and ask for help if you need it.

In

I spelled _____ words correctly.

4E

1. Read the story to your student.

2. Read it together slowly. Have the student look carefully at each word as you read.

3. Together, find all the <u>consonant chunks</u> in the passage and mark them in blue.

In colonial times, people used quill pens to write. A quill is the hollow shaft inside a feather. The tip of the feather is cut to form a point. Then the shaft is filled with ink. Learning to write with a quill pen takes time and practice. After every few words, the pen runs out of ink. Then you must refill it from an inkwell. The ballpoint pens we have today are much easier to use!

Consonant Chunks

ch   gh   ph   sh   th   wh

gn   kn   qu   wr   dg   ck   tch

bb   cc   dd   ff   gg   hh   kk   ll   mm

nn   pp   rr   ss   tt   ww   vv   zz

Section 2: Second Dictation

See if you can write this week's story from dictation without asking for help.

I spelled _____ words correctly.

1. Read the story to your student.

2. Read it together slowly. Have the student look carefully at each word as you read.

3. Together, find and mark all the **vowel chunks** and **consonant chunks**. Use yellow for <u>**vowel chunks**</u> and blue for <u>**consonant chunks**</u>.

As a young boy, Eli Whitney loved to tinker. He loved to see how things worked. When he was older, he invented a cotton gin. With the turn of a crank, steel teeth grabbed the fibers of cotton. The teeth pulled the fibers through holes and left the seeds behind. Before this, people had to separate the seeds by hand. With the gin, cotton could be produced faster. Soon cotton became the main crop of the South.

Vowel Chunks

aa ae ai ao au aw ay

ea ee ei eo ew ey eau

ia ie ii io iu

oa oe oi oo ou ow oy

ua ue ui uo uy

Consonant Chunks

ch gh ph sh th wh

gn kn qu wr dg ck tch

bb cc dd ff gg hh kk ll mm

nn pp rr ss tt ww vv zz

Copy and chunk the story.

As a young boy, Eli Whitney loved

A

to tinker. He loved to see how

t

things worked. When he was older,

t

he invented a cotton gin. With the

h

turn of a crank, steel teeth

t

grabbed the fibers of cotton. The

g

teeth pulled the fibers through

t

holes and left the seeds behind.

h

1. Read the story to your student.

2. Read it together slowly. Have the student look carefully at each word as you read.

3. Together, find and mark all the **vowel chunks** and **consonant chunks**. Use yellow for **vowel chunks** and blue for **consonant chunks**.

As a young boy, Eli Whitney loved to tinker. He loved to see how things worked. When he was older, he invented a cotton gin. With the turn of a crank, steel teeth grabbed the fibers of cotton. The teeth pulled the fibers through holes and left the seeds behind. Before this, people had to separate the seeds by hand. With the gin, cotton could be produced faster. Soon cotton became the main crop of the South.

Vowel Chunks

aa ae ai ao au aw ay

ea ee ei eo ew ey eau

ia ie ii io iu

oa oe oi oo ou ow oy

ua ue ui uo uy

Consonant Chunks

ch gh ph sh th wh

gn kn qu wr dg ck tch

bb cc dd ff gg hh kk ll mm

nn pp rr ss tt ww vv zz

Copy and chunk the story.

With the turn of a crank, steel

W

teeth grabbed the fibers of cotton.

t

The teeth pulled the fibers through

T

holes and left the seeds behind.

h

Before this, people had to separate

B

the seeds by hand. With the gin,

t

cotton could be produced faster.

c

Soon cotton became the main crop

S

of the South.

o

1. Read the story to your student.

2. Read it together slowly. Have the student look carefully at each word as you read.

3. Together, find and mark all the **vowel chunks** and **consonant chunks**. Use yellow for **vowel chunks** and blue for **consonant chunks**.

As a young boy, Eli Whitney loved to tinker. He loved to see how things worked. When he was older, he invented a cotton gin. With the turn of a crank, steel teeth grabbed the fibers of cotton. The teeth pulled the fibers through holes and left the seeds behind. Before this, people had to separate the seeds by hand. With the gin, cotton could be produced faster. Soon cotton became the main crop of the South.

Vowel Chunks

aa ae ai ao au aw ay

ea ee ei eo ew ey eau

ia ie ii io iu

oa oe oi oo ou ow oy

ua ue ui uo uy

Consonant Chunks

ch gh ph sh th wh

gn kn qu wr dg ck tch

bb cc dd ff gg hh kk ll mm

nn pp rr ss tt ww vv zz

Copy and chunk the story.

As a young boy, Eli Whitney loved

A

to tinker. He loved to see how

t

things worked. When he was older,

t

he invented a cotton gin. With the

h

turn of a crank, steel teeth

t

grabbed the fibers of cotton. The

g

teeth pulled the fibers through

t

holes and left the seeds behind.

h

1. Read the story to your student.

2. Read it together slowly. Have the student look carefully at each word as you read.

3. Together, find and mark all the **vowel chunks** and **consonant chunks**. Use yellow for <u>**vowel chunks**</u> and blue for <u>**consonant chunks**</u>.

As a young boy, Eli Whitney loved to tinker. He loved to see how things worked. When he was older, he invented a cotton gin. With the turn of a crank, steel teeth grabbed the fibers of cotton. The teeth pulled the fibers through holes and left the seeds behind. Before this, people had to separate the seeds by hand. With the gin, cotton could be produced faster. Soon cotton became the main crop of the South.

Vowel Chunks

aa ae ai ao au aw ay
ea ee ei eo ew ey eau
ia ie ii io iu
oa oe oi oo ou ow oy
ua ue ui uo uy

Consonant Chunks

ch gh ph sh th wh
gn kn qu wr dg ck tch
bb cc dd ff gg hh kk ll mm
nn pp rr ss tt ww vv zz

Section 2: First Dictation

Write this week's story from dictation. Take your time and ask for help if you need it.

As

I spelled _____ words correctly.

1. Read the story to your student.

2. Read it together slowly. Have the student look carefully at each word as you read.

3. Together, find and mark all the **vowel chunks** and **consonant chunks**. Use yellow for <u>**vowel chunks**</u> and blue for <u>**consonant chunks**</u>.

As a young boy, Eli Whitney loved to tinker. He loved to see how things worked. When he was older, he invented a cotton gin. With the turn of a crank, steel teeth grabbed the fibers of cotton. The teeth pulled the fibers through holes and left the seeds behind. Before this, people had to separate the seeds by hand. With the gin, cotton could be produced faster. Soon cotton became the main crop of the South.

Vowel Chunks

aa ae ai ao au aw ay

ea ee ei eo ew ey eau

ia ie ii io iu

oa oe oi oo ou ow oy

ua ue ui uo uy

Consonant Chunks

ch gh ph sh th wh

gn kn qu wr dg ck tch

bb cc dd ff gg hh kk ll mm

nn pp rr ss tt ww vv zz

Section 2: Second Dictation

See if you can write this week's story from dictation without asking for help.

I spelled _____ words correctly.

1. Read the story to your student.

2. Read it together slowly. Have the student look carefully at each word as you read.

3. Together, find and mark all the **vowel chunks** and **consonant chunks**. Use yellow for **vowel chunks** and blue for **consonant chunks**.

In times past, building a barn by hand was too much work for one family. So they had a barn raising. People from all around would gather at a farm. There might be 100 men working together. Women cooked and served meals. Children helped in small ways. In just a day or two, they could build a large barn! It was hard work, but people had a chance to see and help each other.

Consonant Chunks

ch	gh	ph	sh	th	wh	
gn	kn	qu	wr	dg	ck	tch
bb	cc	dd	ff	gg	hh	kk	ll	mm
nn	pp	rr	ss	tt	ww	vv	zz

Vowel Chunks

aa	ae	ai	ao	au	aw	ay
ea	ee	ei	eo	ew	ey	eau
ia	ie	ii	io	iu		
oa	oe	oi	oo	ou	ow	oy
ua	ue	ui	uo	uy		

Copy and chunk the story.

In times past, building a barn by

I

hand was too much work for one

h

family. So they had a barn raising.

f

People from all around would

P

gather at a farm. There might

g

be 100 men working together.

b

Women cooked and served meals.

W

Children helped in small ways.

C

1. Read the story to your student.

2. Read it together slowly. Have the student look carefully at each word as you read.

3. Together, find and mark all the **vowel chunks** and **consonant chunks**. Use yellow for <u>vowel chunks</u> and blue for <u>consonant chunks</u>.

In times past, building a barn by hand was too much work for one family. So they had a barn raising. People from all around would gather at a farm. There might be 100 men working together. Women cooked and served meals. Children helped in small ways. In just a day or two, they could build a large barn! It was hard work, but people had a chance to see and help each other.

Consonant Chunks

ch	gh	ph	sh	th	wh
gn	kn	qu	wr	dg	ck	tch
bb	cc	dd	ff	gg	hh	kk	ll	mm
nn	pp	rr	ss	tt	ww	vv	zz

Vowel Chunks

aa	ae	ai	ao	au	aw	ay
ea	ee	ei	eo	ew	ey	eau
ia	ie	ii	io	iu		
oa	oe	oi	oo	ou	ow	oy
ua	ue	ui	uo	uy		

Copy and chunk the story.

People from all around would

P

gather at a farm. There might be

g

100 men working together. Women

100

cooked and served meals.

c

Children helped in small ways.

C

In just a day or two, they could

I

build a large barn! It was hard

b

work, but people had a chance

W

to see and help each other.

t

1. Read the story to your student.

2. Read it together slowly. Have the student look carefully at each word as you read.

3. Together, find and mark all the **vowel chunks** and **consonant chunks**. Use yellow for <u>**vowel chunks**</u> and blue for <u>**consonant chunks**</u>.

In times past, building a barn by hand was too much work for one family. So they had a barn raising. People from all around would gather at a farm. There might be 100 men working together. Women cooked and served meals. Children helped in small ways. In just a day or two, they could build a large barn! It was hard work, but people had a chance to see and help each other.

Consonant Chunks

ch   gh   ph   sh   th   wh

gn   kn   qu   wr   dg   ck   tch

bb   cc   dd   ff   gg   hh   kk   ll   mm

nn   pp   rr   ss   tt   ww   vv   zz

Vowel Chunks

aa   ae   ai   ao   au   aw   ay

ea   ee   ei   eo   ew   ey   eau

ia   ie   ii   io   iu

oa   oe   oi   oo   ou   ow   oy

ua   ue   ui   uo   uy

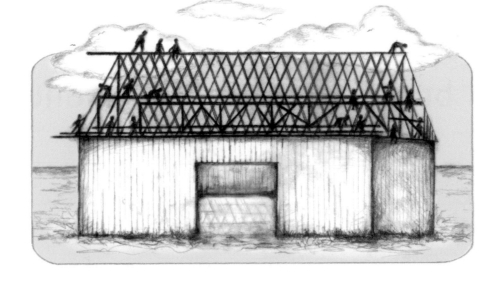

Copy and chunk the story.

In times past, building a barn by

I

hand was too much work for one

h

family. So they had a barn raising.

f

People from all around would

P

gather at a farm. There might

g

be 100 men working together.

b

Women cooked and served meals.

W

Children helped in small ways.

C

1. Read the story to your student.

2. Read it together slowly. Have the student look carefully at each word as you read.

3. Together, find and mark all the **vowel chunks** and **consonant chunks**. Use yellow for **vowel chunks** and blue for **consonant chunks**.

In times past, building a barn by hand was too much work for one family. So they had a barn raising. People from all around would gather at a farm. There might be 100 men working together. Women cooked and served meals. Children helped in small ways. In just a day or two, they could build a large barn! It was hard work, but people had a chance to see and help each other.

Consonant Chunks

ch   gh   ph   sh   th   wh

gn   kn   qu   wr   dg   ck   tch

bb   cc   dd   ff   gg   hh   kk   ll   mm

nn   pp   rr   ss   tt   ww   vv   zz

Vowel Chunks

aa   ae   ai   ao   au   aw   ay

ea   ee   ei   eo   ew   ey   eau

ia   ie   ii   io   iu

oa   oe   oi   oo   ou   ow   oy

ua   ue   ui   uo   uy

Write this week's story from dictation. Take your time and ask for help if you need it.

In

I spelled _____ words correctly.

6E

Section 1: Vowel and Consonant Chunks

1. Read the story to your student.

2. Read it together slowly. Have the student look carefully at each word as you read.

3. Together, find and mark all the **vowel chunks** and **consonant chunks**. Use yellow for <u>**vowel chunks**</u> and blue for <u>**consonant chunks**</u>.

In times past, building a barn by hand was too much work for one family. So they had a barn raising. People from all around would gather at a farm. There might be 100 men working together. Women cooked and served meals. Children helped in small ways. In just a day or two, they could build a large barn! It was hard work, but people had a chance to see and help each other.

Consonant Chunks

ch gh ph sh th wh
gn kn qu wr dg ck tch
bb cc dd ff gg hh kk ll mm
nn pp rr ss tt ww vv zz

Vowel Chunks

aa ae ai ao au aw ay
ea ee ei eo ew ey eau
ia ie ii io iu
oa oe oi oo ou ow oy
ua ue ui uo uy

Section 2: Second Dictation

See if you can write this week's story from dictation without asking for help.

I spelled _____ words correctly.

1. Read the story to your student.

2. Read it together slowly. Have the student look carefully at each word as you read.

3. Go to the instructions for Lesson 7 in the *Handbook* for examples of how Bossy *r* changes the sound of a vowel. Together, look for <u>**Bossy *r* chunks**</u> and mark them in purple.

It took Patrick a while to figure out what kind of work to do. He tried farming, but his farm had poor soil. He started a store, but that did not go well. Finally he became a lawyer. In time, he became a great speaker. He gave stirring speeches about wanting freedom from England. Patrick Henry is remembered for ending one speech with the line, "Give me liberty, or give me death!"

Bossy r Chunks
ar   er   ir   or   ur

Copy the story. Mark all the Bossy *r* chunks on your copy.

It took Patrick a while to figure

out what kind of work to do.

He tried farming, but his farm

had poor soil. He started a store,

but that did not go well. Finally

he became a lawyer. In time, he

became a great speaker. He gave

stirring speeches about wanting

freedom from England.

1. Read the story to your student.

2. Read it together slowly. Have the student look carefully at each word as you read.

3. Help your student find and mark the **<u>Bossy _r_ chunks</u>** in purple.

It took Patrick a while to figure out what kind of work to do. He tried farming, but his farm had poor soil. He started a store, but that did not go well. Finally he became a lawyer. In time, he became a great speaker. He gave stirring speeches about wanting freedom from England. Patrick Henry is remembered for ending one speech with the line, "Give me liberty, or give me death!"

Bossy r Chunks
_ar   er   ir   or   ur_

Copy the story. Mark all the Bossy *r* chunks on your copy.

He started a store, but that did

not go well. Finally he became

a lawyer. In time, he became a

great speaker. He gave stirring

speeches about wanting freedom

from England. Patrick Henry is

remembered for ending one

speech with the line, "Give me

liberty, or give me death!"

1. Read the story to your student.

2. Read it together slowly. Have the student look carefully at each word as you read.

3. Help your student find and mark the **Bossy *r* chunks** in purple.

It took Patrick a while to figure out what kind of work to do. He tried farming, but his farm had poor soil. He started a store, but that did not go well. Finally he became a lawyer. In time, he became a great speaker. He gave stirring speeches about wanting freedom from England. Patrick Henry is remembered for ending one speech with the line, "Give me liberty, or give me death!"

Bossy *r* Chunks
ar   er   ir   or   ur

Copy the story. Mark all the Bossy *r* chunks on your copy.

It took Patrick a while to figure

I

out what kind of work to do.

o

He tried farming, but his farm

H

had poor soil. He started a store,

h

but that did not go well. Finally

b

he became a lawyer. In time, he

h

became a great speaker. He gave

b

stirring speeches about wanting

s

freedom from England.

f

1. Read the story to your student.

2. Read it together slowly. Have the student look carefully at each word as you read.

3. Help your student find and mark the <u>**Bossy *r* chunks**</u> in purple.

It took Patrick a while to figure out what kind of work to do. He tried farming, but his farm had poor soil. He started a store, but that did not go well. Finally he became a lawyer. In time, he became a great speaker. He gave stirring speeches about wanting freedom from England. Patrick Henry is remembered for ending one speech with the line, "Give me liberty, or give me death!"

Bossy r Chunks
ar   er   ir   or   ur

Section 2: First Dictation

Write this week's story from dictation. Take your time and ask for help if you need it.

It

I spelled _____ words correctly.

1. Read the story to your student.

2. Read it together slowly. Have the student look carefully at each word as you read.

3. Help your student find and mark the <u>**Bossy *r* chunks**</u> in purple.

It took Patrick a while to figure out what kind of work to do. He tried farming, but his farm had poor soil. He started a store, but that did not go well. Finally he became a lawyer. In time, he became a great speaker. He gave stirring speeches about wanting freedom from England. Patrick Henry is remembered for ending one speech with the line, "Give me liberty, or give me death!"

Bossy r Chunks
ar er ir or ur

Section 2: Second Dictation

See if you can write this week's story from dictation without asking for help.

_____

_____

_____

_____

_____

_____

_____

_____

_____

_____

_____

_____

_____

_____

_____

_____

_____

_____

_____

_____

_____

_____

_____

_____

_____

_____

_____

_____

_____

I spelled _____ words correctly.

1. Read the story to your student.

2. Read it together slowly. Have the student look carefully at each word as you read.

3. Together, look for **Bossy *r* chunks** and mark them in purple.

In 1775 David Bushnell built a one-man submarine. He called it the *Turtle* because of the way it looked. He used it to target enemy ships. His plan was to put a bomb on the hull of a large ship. Then he would escape through the murky water before the bomb blew up. His idea did not work very well. The *Turtle* is remembered as the first submarine used in a war.

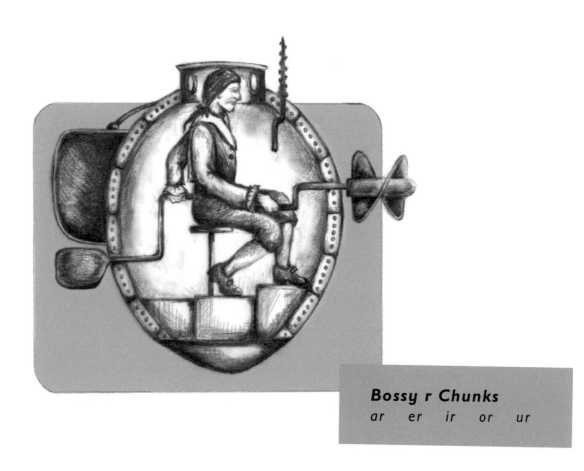

Bossy r Chunks
ar   er   ir   or   ur

Copy the story. Mark all the Bossy *r* chunks on your copy.

In 1775 David Bushnell built a

l

one-man submarine. He called it

o

the Turtle because of the way it

t

looked. He used it to target

l

enemy ships. His plan was to

e

put a bomb on the hull of a

p

large ship. Then he would escape

l

through the murky water

t

before the bomb blew up.

b

1. Read the story to your student.

2. Read it together slowly. Have the student look carefully at each word as you read.

3. Together, look for **Bossy _r_ chunks** and mark them in purple.

In 1775 David Bushnell built a one-man submarine. He called it the _Turtle_ because of the way it looked. He used it to target enemy ships. His plan was to put a bomb on the hull of a large ship. Then he would escape through the murky water before the bomb blew up. His idea did not work very well. The _Turtle_ is remembered as the first submarine used in a war.

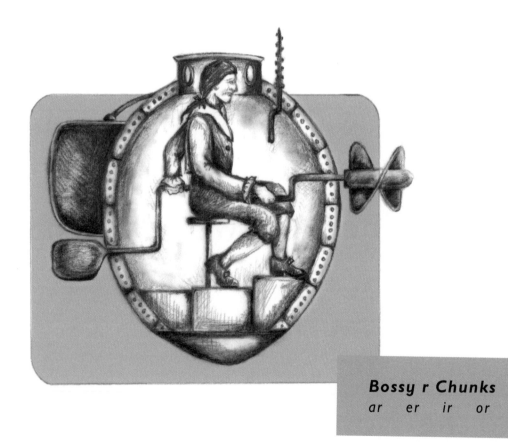

Bossy r Chunks
_ar   er   ir   or   ur_

Copy the story. Mark all the Bossy *r* chunks on your copy.

He used it to target enemy ships.

H

His plan was to put a bomb on

H

the hull of a large ship. Then he

t

would escape through the murky

W

water before the bomb blew up.

W

His idea did not work very well.

H

The Turtle is remembered as the

T

first submarine used in a war.

f

1. Read the story to your student.

2. Read it together slowly. Have the student look carefully at each word as you read.

3. Together, look for **Bossy *r* chunks** and mark them in purple.

In 1775 David Bushnell built a one-man submarine. He called it the *Turtle* because of the way it looked. He used it to target enemy ships. His plan was to put a bomb on the hull of a large ship. Then he would escape through the murky water before the bomb blew up. His idea did not work very well. The *Turtle* is remembered as the first submarine used in a war.

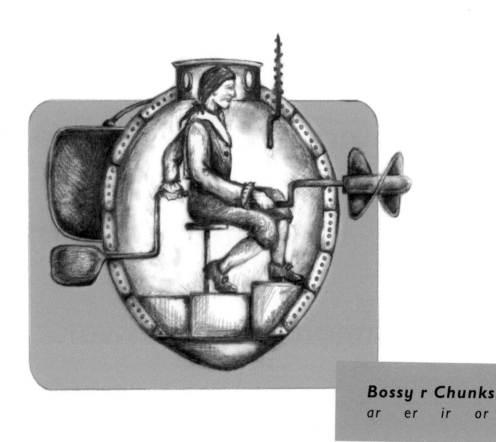

Bossy r Chunks
ar   er   ir   or   ur

Copy the story. Mark all the Bossy *r* chunks on your copy.

In 1775 David Bushnell built a

I

one-man submarine. He called it

o

the Turtle because of the way it

t

looked. He used it to target

l

enemy ships. His plan was to

e

put a bomb on the hull of a

p

large ship. Then he would escape

l

through the murky water

t

before the bomb blew up.

b

1. Read the story to your student.

2. Read it together slowly. Have the student look carefully at each word as you read.

3. Together, look for **Bossy *r* chunks** and mark them in purple.

In 1775 David Bushnell built a one-man submarine. He called it the *Turtle* because of the way it looked. He used it to target enemy ships. His plan was to put a bomb on the hull of a large ship. Then he would escape through the murky water before the bomb blew up. His idea did not work very well. The *Turtle* is remembered as the first submarine used in a war.

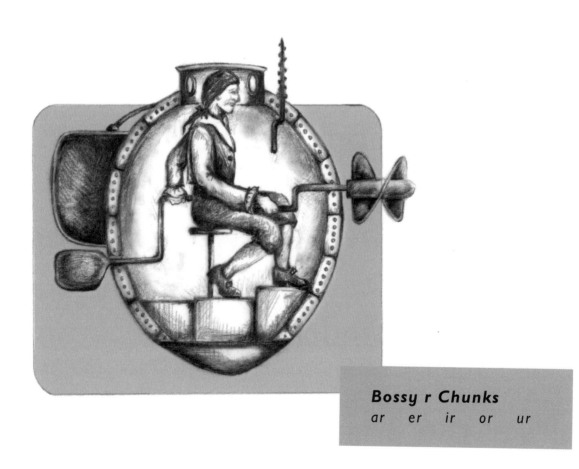

Bossy r Chunks
ar   er   ir   or   ur

Section 2: First Dictation

Write this week's story from dictation. Take your time and ask for help if you need it.

In

I spelled _____ words correctly.   **81**

1. Read the story to your student.

2. Read it together slowly. Have the student look carefully at each word as you read.

3. Together, look for **Bossy *r* chunks** and mark them in purple.

In 1775 David Bushnell built a one-man submarine. He called it the *Turtle* because of the way it looked. He used it to target enemy ships. His plan was to put a bomb on the hull of a large ship. Then he would escape through the murky water before the bomb blew up. His idea did not work very well. The *Turtle* is remembered as the first submarine used in a war.

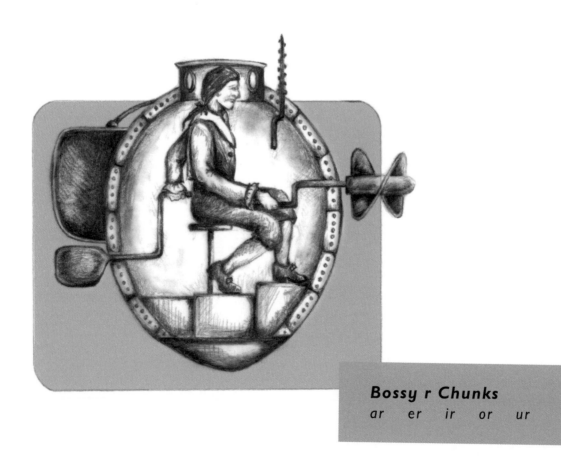

Bossy r Chunks
ar   er   ir   or   ur

See if you can write this week's story from dictation without asking for help.

I spelled _____ words correctly.

1. Read the story to your student.

2. Read it together slowly. Have the student look carefully at each word as you read.

3. This week, look for all the letter patterns studied so far. Mark <u>**vowel chunks**</u> in yellow, <u>**consonant chunks**</u> in blue, and <u>**Bossy *r* chunks**</u> in purple. The word *soldier* has overlapping chunks. We suggest that you have your student mark the **vowel chunk** rather than the **Bossy *r* chunk**.

A few women helped fight in the Revolutionary War. Soldiers fighting battles need water. Often a woman would run back and forth from a spring. In one battle, a soldier fell to the ground. His wife, Mary Hays, dropped her pitcher. She took over firing the cannon. Over and over she loaded and fired. Suddenly a cannon ball whizzed right between her legs! It tore the bottom of her skirt, but she was not hurt. She kept on fighting.

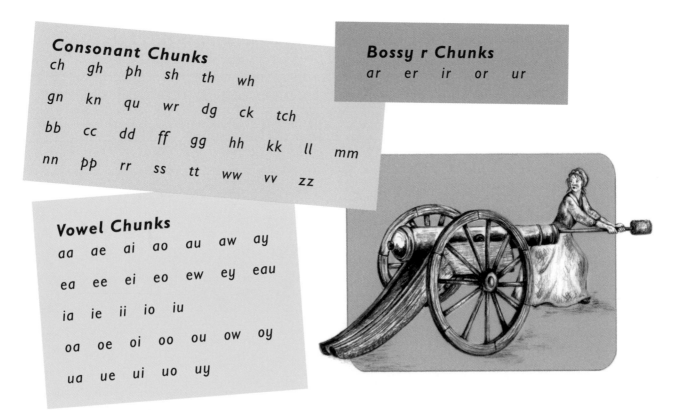

Consonant Chunks

ch   gh   ph   sh   th   wh

gn   kn   qu   wr   dg   ck   tch

bb   cc   dd   ff   gg   hh   kk   ll   mm

nn   pp   rr   ss   tt   ww   vv   zz

Bossy r Chunks

ar   er   ir   or   ur

Vowel Chunks

aa   ae   ai   ao   au   aw   ay

ea   ee   ei   eo   ew   ey   eau

ia   ie   ii   io   iu

oa   oe   oi   oo   ou   ow   oy

ua   ue   ui   uo   uy

Copy and chunk the story.

A few women helped fight in
A

the Revolutionary War. Soldiers
t

fighting battles need water. Often
f

a woman would run back and
a

forth from a spring. In one battle,
f

a soldier fell to the ground. His
a

wife, Mary Hays, dropped her
W

pitcher. She took over firing the
P

cannon.
C

1. Read the story to your student.

2. Read it together slowly. Have the student look carefully at each word as you read.

3. Together, mark **vowel chunks** in yellow, **consonant chunks** in blue, and **Bossy _r_ chunks** in purple.

A few women helped fight in the Revolutionary War. Soldiers fighting battles need water. Often a woman would run back and forth from a spring. In one battle, a soldier fell to the ground. His wife, Mary Hays, dropped her pitcher. She took over firing the cannon. Over and over she loaded and fired. Suddenly a cannon ball whizzed right between her legs! It tore the bottom of her skirt, but she was not hurt. She kept on fighting.

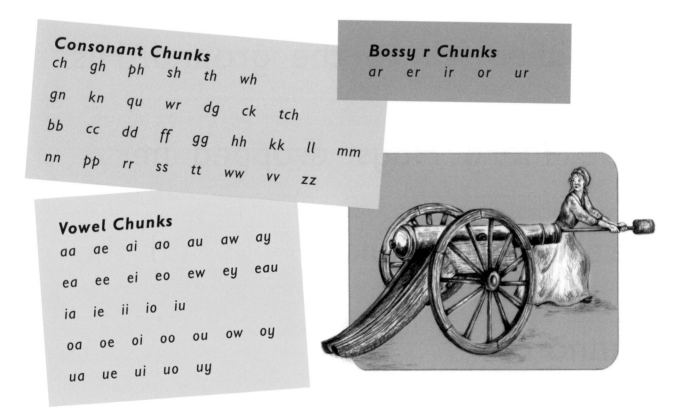

Consonant Chunks

ch   gh   ph   sh   th   wh

gn   kn   qu   wr   dg   ck   tch

bb   cc   dd   ff   gg   hh   kk   ll   mm

nn   pp   rr   ss   tt   ww   vv   zz

Bossy r Chunks

ar   er   ir   or   ur

Vowel Chunks

aa   ae   ai   ao   au   aw   ay

ea   ee   ei   eo   ew   ey   eau

ia   ie   ii   io   iu

oa   oe   oi   oo   ou   ow   oy

ua   ue   ui   uo   uy

Copy and chunk the story.

In one battle, a soldier fell to

I

the ground. His wife, Mary Hays,

t

dropped her pitcher. She took over

d

firing the cannon. Over and over

f

she loaded and fired. Suddenly a

s

cannon ball whizzed right between

c

her legs! It tore the bottom of

h

her skirt, but she was not hurt.

h

She kept on fighting.

S

1. Read the story to your student.

2. Read it together slowly. Have the student look carefully at each word as you read.

3. Together, mark **vowel chunks** in yellow, **consonant chunks** in blue, and **Bossy *r* chunks** in purple.

A few women helped fight in the Revolutionary War. Soldiers fighting battles need water. Often a woman would run back and forth from a spring. In one battle, a soldier fell to the ground. His wife, Mary Hays, dropped her pitcher. She took over firing the cannon. Over and over she loaded and fired. Suddenly a cannon ball whizzed right between her legs! It tore the bottom of her skirt, but she was not hurt. She kept on fighting.

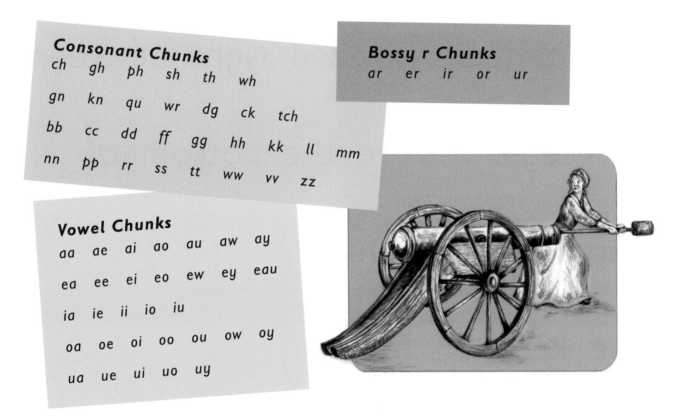

Consonant Chunks

ch gh ph sh th wh
gn kn qu wr dg ck tch
bb cc dd ff gg hh kk ll mm
nn pp rr ss tt ww vv zz

Bossy r Chunks

ar er ir or ur

Vowel Chunks

aa ae ai ao au aw ay
ea ee ei eo ew ey eau
ia ie ii io iu
oa oe oi oo ou ow oy
ua ue ui uo uy

Section 2: Copywork

Copy and chunk the story.

A few women helped fight in

A

the Revolutionary War. Soldiers

t

fighting battles need water. Often

f

a woman would run back and

a

forth from a spring. In one battle,

f

a soldier fell to the ground. His

a

wife, Mary Hays, dropped her

w

pitcher. She took over firing the

P

cannon.

c

1. Read the story to your student.

2. Read it together slowly. Have the student look carefully at each word as you read.

3. Together, mark **vowel chunks** in yellow, **consonant chunks** in blue, and **Bossy *r* chunks** in purple.

A few women helped fight in the Revolutionary War. Soldiers fighting battles need water. Often a woman would run back and forth from a spring. In one battle, a soldier fell to the ground. His wife, Mary Hays, dropped her pitcher. She took over firing the cannon. Over and over she loaded and fired. Suddenly a cannon ball whizzed right between her legs! It tore the bottom of her skirt, but she was not hurt. She kept on fighting.

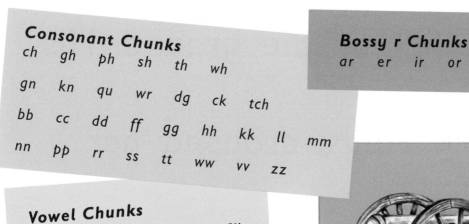

Consonant Chunks

ch   gh   ph   sh   th   wh
gn   kn   qu   wr   dg   ck   tch
bb   cc   dd   ff   gg   hh   kk   ll   mm
nn   pp   rr   ss   tt   ww   vv   zz

Bossy r Chunks

ar   er   ir   or   ur

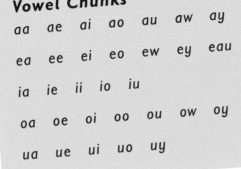

Vowel Chunks

aa   ae   ai   ao   au   aw   ay
ea   ee   ei   eo   ew   ey   eau
ia   ie   ii   io   iu
oa   oe   oi   oo   ou   ow   oy
ua   ue   ui   uo   uy

Section 2: First Dictation

Write this week's story from dictation. Take your time and ask for help if you need it.

A
_____

1. Read the story to your student.

2. Read it together slowly. Have the student look carefully at each word as you read.

3. Together, mark **vowel chunks** in yellow, **consonant chunks** in blue, and **Bossy _r_ chunks** in purple.

A few women helped fight in the Revolutionary War. Soldiers fighting battles need water. Often a woman would run back and forth from a spring. In one battle, a soldier fell to the ground. His wife, Mary Hays, dropped her pitcher. She took over firing the cannon. Over and over she loaded and fired. Suddenly a cannon ball whizzed right between her legs! It tore the bottom of her skirt, but she was not hurt. She kept on fighting.

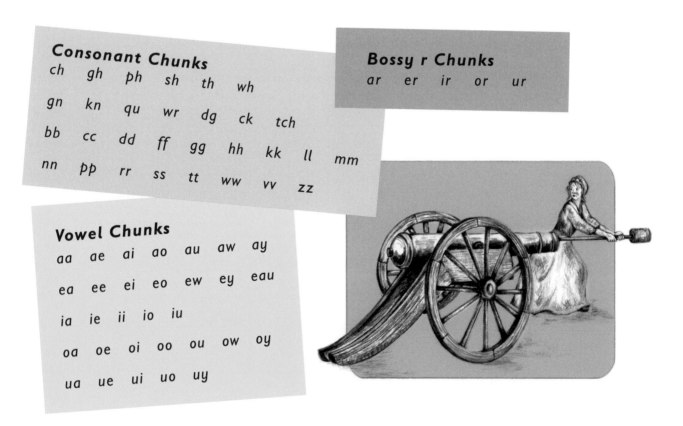

Consonant Chunks

ch gh ph sh th wh
gn kn qu wr dg ck tch
bb cc dd ff gg hh kk ll mm
nn pp rr ss tt ww vv zz

Bossy r Chunks

ar er ir or ur

Vowel Chunks

aa ae ai ao au aw ay
ea ee ei eo ew ey eau
ia ie ii io iu
oa oe oi oo ou ow oy
ua ue ui uo uy

Section 2: Second Dictation

See if you can write this week's story from dictation without asking for help.

I spelled _____ words correctly.

1. Read the story to your student.

2. Read it together slowly. Have the student look carefully at each word as you read.

3. Together, mark the <u>vowel chunks</u>, <u>consonant chunks</u>, and <u>**Bossy *r* chunks**</u>. Be sure to use the correct color for each letter pattern.

Annie Oakley was skilled with a rifle. As a teenager, she shot game to feed her family. She sold the extra. Soon she paid off her family's debt. People noticed her shooting skill. She became a sharpshooter in Buffalo Bill's Wild West Show. She was only five feet tall, so she was called Little Sure Shot. She performed with her husband and set many records for shooting.

Bossy *r* Chunks

ar   er   ir   or   ur

Vowel Chunks

aa   ae   ai   ao   au   aw   ay

ea   ee   ei   eo   ew   ey   eau

ia   ie   ii   io   iu

oa   oe   oi   oo   ou   ow   oy

ua   ue   ui   uo   uy

Consonant Chunks

ch   gh   ph   sh   th   wh

gn   kn   qu   wr   dg   ck   tch

bb   cc   dd   ff   gg   hh   kk   ll   mm

nn   pp   rr   ss   tt   ww   vv   zz

Copy and chunk the story.

Annie Oakley was skilled with

A

a rifle. As a teenager, she shot

a

game to feed her family. She sold

g

the extra. Soon she paid off her

t

family's debt. People noticed her

f

shooting skill. She became a

s

sharpshooter in Buffalo Bill's Wild

s

West Show.

W

1. Read the story to your student.

2. Read it together slowly. Have the student look carefully at each word as you read.

3. Together, mark the **vowel chunks**, **consonant chunks**, and **Bossy *r* chunks**. Be sure to use the correct color for each letter pattern.

Annie Oakley was skilled with a rifle. As a teenager, she shot game to feed her family. She sold the extra. Soon she paid off her family's debt. People noticed her shooting skill. She became a sharpshooter in Buffalo Bill's Wild West Show. She was only five feet tall, so she was called Little Sure Shot. She performed with her husband and set many records for shooting.

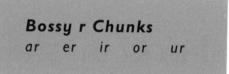

Bossy r Chunks

ar   er   ir   or   ur

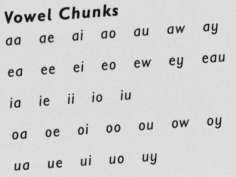

Vowel Chunks

aa	ae	ai	ao	au	aw	ay
ea	ee	ei	eo	ew	ey	eau
ia	ie	ii	io	iu		
oa	oe	oi	oo	ou	ow	oy
ua	ue	ui	uo	uy		

Consonant Chunks

ch	gh	ph	sh	th	wh	
gn	kn	qu	wr	dg	ck	tch
bb	cc	dd	ff	gg	hh	kk	ll	mm
nn	pp	rr	ss	tt	ww	vv	zz

Copy and chunk the story.

She sold the extra. Soon she paid

S

off her family's debt. People

o

noticed her shooting skill. She

n

became a sharpshooter in Buffalo

b

Bill's Wild West Show. She was

B

only five feet tall, so she was

o

called Little Sure Shot. She

c

performed with her husband and

P

set many records for shooting.

s

1. Read the story to your student.

2. Read it together slowly. Have the student look carefully at each word as you read.

3. Together, mark the <u>**vowel chunks**</u>, <u>**consonant chunks**</u>, and <u>**Bossy _r_ chunks**</u>. Be sure to use the correct color for each letter pattern.

Annie Oakley was skilled with a rifle. As a teenager, she shot game to feed her family. She sold the extra. Soon she paid off her family's debt. People noticed her shooting skill. She became a sharpshooter in Buffalo Bill's Wild West Show. She was only five feet tall, so she was called Little Sure Shot. She performed with her husband and set many records for shooting.

Bossy r Chunks

ar   er   ir   or   ur

Vowel Chunks

aa ae ai ao au aw ay

ea ee ei eo ew ey eau

ia ie ii io iu

oa oe oi oo ou ow oy

ua ue ui uo uy

Consonant Chunks

ch   gh   ph   sh   th   wh

gn   kn   qu   wr   dg   ck   tch

bb   cc   dd   ff   gg   hh   kk   ll   mm

nn   pp   rr   ss   tt   ww   vv   zz

Copy and chunk the story.

Annie Oakley was skilled with

A

a rifle. As a teenager, she shot

a

game to feed her family. She sold

g

the extra. Soon she paid off her

t

family's debt. People noticed her

f

shooting skill. She became a

s

sharpshooter in Buffalo Bill's Wild

s

West Show.

W

1. Read the story to your student.

2. Read it together slowly. Have the student look carefully at each word as you read.

3. Together, mark the **vowel chunks**, **consonant chunks**, and **Bossy *r* chunks**. Be sure to use the correct color for each letter pattern.

Annie Oakley was skilled with a rifle. As a teenager, she shot game to feed her family. She sold the extra. Soon she paid off her family's debt. People noticed her shooting skill. She became a sharpshooter in Buffalo Bill's Wild West Show. She was only five feet tall, so she was called Little Sure Shot. She performed with her husband and set many records for shooting.

Bossy r Chunks
ar   er   ir   or   ur

Vowel Chunks
aa   ae   ai   ao   au   aw   ay
ea   ee   ei   eo   ew   ey   eau
ia   ie   ii   io   iu
oa   oe   oi   oo   ou   ow   oy
ua   ue   ui   uo   uy

Consonant Chunks
ch   gh   ph   sh   th   wh
gn   kn   qu   wr   dg   ck   tch
bb   cc   dd   ff   gg   hh   kk   ll   mm
nn   pp   rr   ss   tt   ww   vv   zz

Write this week's story from dictation. Take your time and ask for help if you need it.

Annie

I spelled _____ words correctly.

10E

1. Read the story to your student.

2. Read it together slowly. Have the student look carefully at each word as you read.

3. Together, mark the <u>**vowel chunks**</u>, <u>**consonant chunks**</u>, and <u>**Bossy r chunks**</u>. Be sure to use the correct color for each letter pattern.

Annie Oakley was skilled with a rifle. As a teenager, she shot game to feed her family. She sold the extra. Soon she paid off her family's debt. People noticed her shooting skill. She became a sharpshooter in Buffalo Bill's Wild West Show. She was only five feet tall, so she was called Little Sure Shot. She performed with her husband and set many records for shooting.

Bossy r Chunks
ar   er   ir   or   ur

Vowel Chunks
aa ae ai ao au aw ay
ea ee ei eo ew ey eau
ia ie ii io iu
oa oe oi oo ou ow oy
ua ue ui uo uy

Consonant Chunks
ch gh ph sh th wh
gn kn qu wr dg ck tch
bb cc dd ff gg hh kk ll mm
nn pp rr ss tt ww vv zz

Section 2: Second Dictation

See if you can write this week's story from dictation without asking for help.

I spelled _____ words correctly.

1. Read the story to your student.

2. Read it together slowly. Have the student look carefully at each word as you read.

3. In this lesson, you will be finding three new letter patterns. They are **Tricky *y* Guy**, **endings**, and **silent letters**. We recommend that you mark **endings** before **silent letters**. Look for **silent letters** that are not part of **endings** or other chunks.

4. Mark <u>**Tricky y Guy**</u> in green, <u>**endings**</u> in pink or red, and <u>**silent letters**</u> in orange.

5. Refer to the *Handbook* for more information about these letter patterns.

Samuel Morse loved painting. He painted pictures of famous people. Later in life he tried to find a faster way to send messages. He invented a telegraph. It used Morse code, a system of dots and dashes. Each letter and number had its own code. Messages that would have taken weeks to send by mail could now be sent quickly over wires.

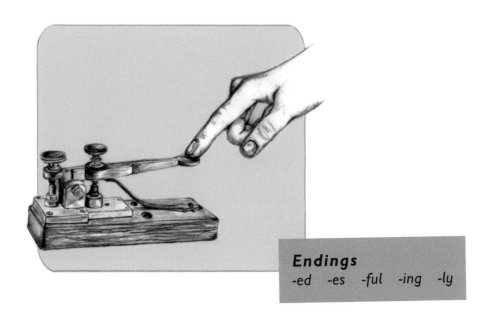

Endings
-ed -es -ful -ing -ly

Copy and chunk the story.

Samuel Morse loved painting.

S

He painted pictures of famous

H

people. Later in life he tried to

P

find a faster way to send

f

messages. He invented a telegraph.

m

It used Morse code, a system

I

# of dots and dashes. Each letter

o

and number had its own code.

a

1. Read the story to your student.

2. Read it together slowly. Have the student look carefully at each word as you read.

3. Mark **Tricky *y* Guy** in green, **endings** in pink or red, and **silent letters** in orange.

Samuel Morse loved painting. He painted pictures of famous people. Later in life he tried to find a faster way to send messages. He invented a telegraph. It used Morse code, a system of dots and dashes. Each letter and number had its own code. Messages that would have taken weeks to send by mail could now be sent quickly over wires.

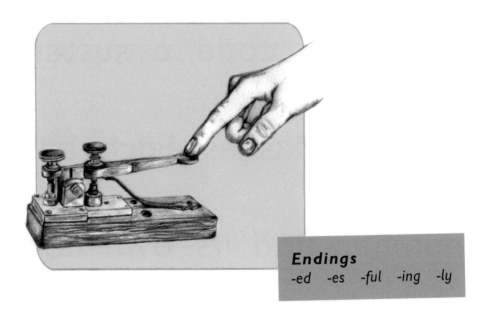

Endings
-ed -es -ful -ing -ly

Copy and chunk the story.

Later in life he tried to find a

L

faster way to send messages.

f

He invented a telegraph. It used

H

Morse code, a system of dots and

M

dashes. Each letter and number

d

had its own code. Messages that

h

would have taken weeks to send

w

by mail could now be sent quickly

b

over wires.

o

1. Read the story to your student.

2. Read it together slowly. Have the student look carefully at each word as you read.

3. Mark **Tricky *y* Guy** in green, <u>endings</u> in pink or red, and <u>silent letters</u> in orange.

Samuel Morse loved painting. He painted pictures of famous people. Later in life he tried to find a faster way to send messages. He invented a telegraph. It used Morse code, a system of dots and dashes. Each letter and number had its own code. Messages that would have taken weeks to send by mail could now be sent quickly over wires.

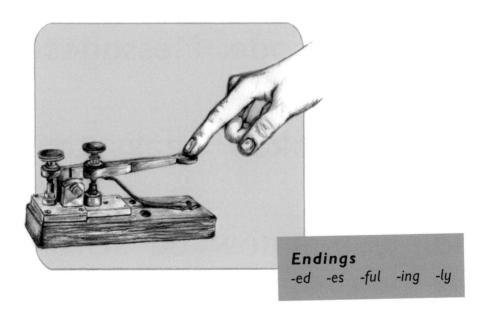

Endings
-ed -es -ful -ing -ly

Copy and chunk the story.

Samuel Morse loved painting.

S

He painted pictures of famous

H

people. Later in life he tried to

P

find a faster way to send

f

messages. He invented a telegraph.

m

It used Morse code, a system

I

of dots and dashes. Each letter

o

and number had its own code.

a

1. Read the story to your student.

2. Read it together slowly. Have the student look carefully at each word as you read.

3. Mark **Tricky _y_ Guy** in green, **endings** in pink or red, and **silent letters** in orange.

Samuel Morse loved painting. He painted pictures of famous people. Later in life he tried to find a faster way to send messages. He invented a telegraph. It used Morse code, a system of dots and dashes. Each letter and number had its own code. Messages that would have taken weeks to send by mail could now be sent quickly over wires.

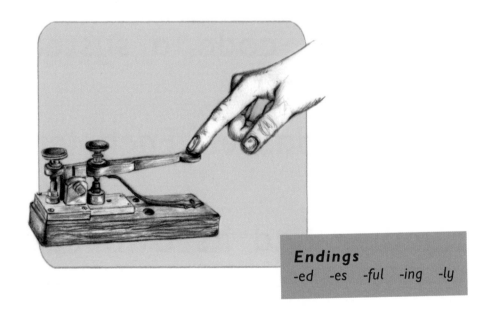

Endings
-ed   -es   -ful   -ing   -ly

Section 2: First Dictation

Write this week's story from dictation. Take your time and ask for help if you need it.

Samuel

1. Read the story to your student.

2. Read it together slowly. Have the student look carefully at each word as you read.

3. Mark **Tricky *y* Guy** in green, **endings** in pink or red, and **silent letters** in orange.

Samuel Morse loved painting. He painted pictures of famous people. Later in life he tried to find a faster way to send messages. He invented a telegraph. It used Morse code, a system of dots and dashes. Each letter and number had its own code. Messages that would have taken weeks to send by mail could now be sent quickly over wires.

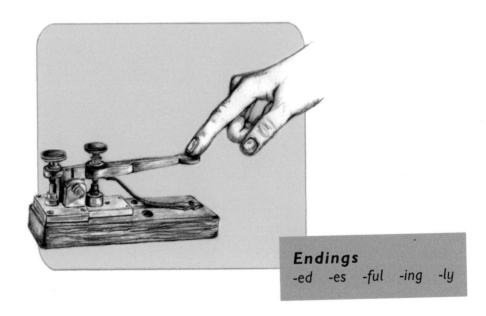

Endings
-ed -es -ful -ing -ly

Section 2: Second Dictation

See if you can write this week's story from dictation without asking for help.

I spelled ______ words correctly.

1. Read the story to your student.

2. Read it together slowly. Have the student look carefully at each word as you read.

3. Mark **Tricky *y* Guy** in green, **endings** in pink or red, and **silent letters** in orange.

Twenty thousand men spent six years building a railroad. Some started in Iowa and headed west. Others started in California and worked east. By 1869 the last spike was finally pounded into place. The East and West were linked. After that, many more railroads were built. The railroads joined every part of the country. The folk song "I've Been Working on the Railroad" became very popular.

Endings
-ed   -es   -ful   -ing   -ly

Copy and chunk the story.

Twenty thousand men spent six

T

years building a railroad. Some

y

started in Iowa and headed west.

s

Others started in California

O

and worked east. By 1869 the

a

last spike was finally pounded

l

into place. The East and West

i

were linked. After that, many

w

more railroads were built.

m

1. Read the story to your student.

2. Read it together slowly. Have the student look carefully at each word as you read.

3. Mark **Tricky *y* Guy** in green, <u>endings</u> in pink or red, and <u>silent letters</u> in orange.

Twenty thousand men spent six years building a railroad. Some started in Iowa and headed west. Others started in California and worked east. By 1869 the last spike was finally pounded into place. The East and West were linked. After that, many more railroads were built. The railroads joined every part of the country. The folk song "I've Been Working on the Railroad" became very popular.

Endings
-ed   -es   -ful   -ing   -ly

Copy and chunk the story.

By **1869** the last spike was

B

finally pounded into place.

f

The East and West were linked.

T

After that, many more railroads

A

were built. The railroads joined

w

every part of the country. The

e

folk song "I've Been Working on

f

the Railroad" became very popular.

t

1. Read the story to your student.

2. Read it together slowly. Have the student look carefully at each word as you read.

3. Mark **Tricky _y_ Guy** in green, **endings** in pink or red, and **silent letters** in orange.

Twenty thousand men spent six years building a railroad. Some started in Iowa and headed west. Others started in California and worked east. By 1869 the last spike was finally pounded into place. The East and West were linked. After that, many more railroads were built. The railroads joined every part of the country. The folk song "I've Been Working on the Railroad" became very popular.

Endings
-ed   -es   -ful   -ing   -ly

Copy and chunk the story.

Twenty thousand men spent six

T

years building a railroad. Some

y

started in Iowa and headed west.

s

Others started in California

O

and worked east. By 1869 the

a

last spike was finally pounded

l

into place. The East and West

i

were linked. After that, many

w

more railroads were built.

m

1. Read the story to your student.

2. Read it together slowly. Have the student look carefully at each word as you read.

3. Mark **Tricky *y* Guy** in green, **endings** in pink or red, and **silent letters** in orange.

Twenty thousand men spent six years building a railroad. Some started in Iowa and headed west. Others started in California and worked east. By 1869 the last spike was finally pounded into place. The East and West were linked. After that, many more railroads were built. The railroads joined every part of the country. The folk song "I've Been Working on the Railroad" became very popular.

Endings
-ed -es -ful -ing -ly

Section 2: First Dictation

Write this week's story from dictation. Take your time and ask for help if you need it.

Twenty

I spelled _____ words correctly.

1. Read the story to your student.

2. Read it together slowly. Have the student look carefully at each word as you read.

3. Mark **Tricky y Guy** in green, **endings** in pink or red, and **silent letters** in orange.

Twenty thousand men spent six years building a railroad.
Some started in Iowa and headed west. Others started
in California and worked east. By 1869 the last spike was
finally pounded into place. The East and West were linked.
After that, many more railroads were built. The railroads
joined every part of the country. The folk song "I've Been
Working on the Railroad" became very popular.

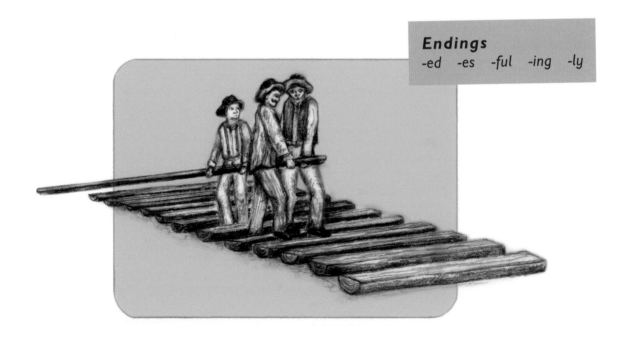

Endings
-ed   -es   -ful   -ing   -ly

See if you can write this week's story from dictation without asking for help.

I spelled _____ words correctly.

1. Read the story to your student.

2. Read it together slowly. Have the student look carefully at each word as you read.

3. This week you and your student will be looking for and marking all six letter patterns that you have learned. They are **vowel chunks** (yellow), **consonant chunks** (blue), **Bossy _r_ chunks** (purple), **Tricky _y_ Guy** (green), **endings** (pink or red), and **silent letters** (orange).

Would it explode? Would it catch fire? Would it sink? Many people on the dock didn't think the new steamboat would go anywhere. The paddle wheel churned, and smoke puffed. The steamboat began to move steadily up the Hudson River. It cruised along, passing all the other boats as though they were standing still. Robert Fulton and his partner didn't invent the steamboat. They helped to make it practical. Before railroads, rivers were the highways of the country.

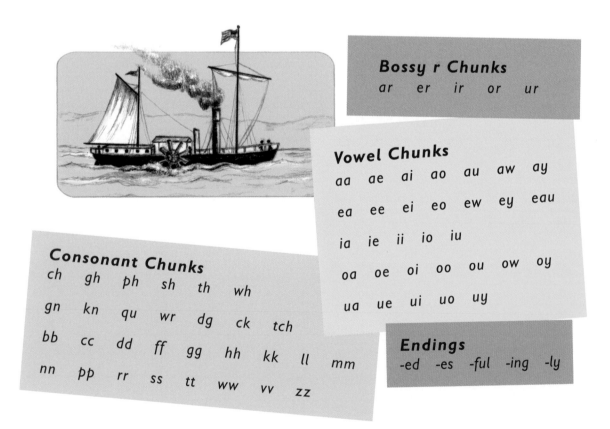

Bossy r Chunks

ar er ir or ur

Vowel Chunks

aa ae ai ao au aw ay

ea ee ei eo ew ey eau

ia ie ii io iu

oa oe oi oo ou ow oy

ua ue ui uo uy

Consonant Chunks

ch gh ph sh th wh

gn kn qu wr dg ck tch

bb cc dd ff gg hh kk ll mm

nn pp rr ss tt ww vv zz

Endings

-ed -es -ful -ing -ly

Copy and chunk the story.

Would it explode? Would it catch

W

fire? Would it sink? Many people

f

on the dock didn't think the new

o

steamboat would go anywhere.

s

The paddle wheel churned, and

T

smoke puffed. The steamboat

s

began to move steadily up the

b

Hudson River.

H

1. Read the story to your student.

2. Read it together slowly. Have the student look carefully at each word as you read.

3. Together, mark the <u>**vowel chunks**</u> (yellow), <u>**consonant chunks**</u> (blue), <u>**Bossy *r* chunks**</u> (purple), <u>**Tricky *y* Guy**</u> (green), <u>**endings**</u> (pink or red), and <u>**silent letters**</u> (orange).

Would it explode? Would it catch fire? Would it sink?
Many people on the dock didn't think the new steamboat
would go anywhere. The paddle wheel churned, and smoke
puffed. The steamboat began to move steadily up the Hudson
River. It cruised along, passing all the other boats as though
they were standing still. Robert Fulton and his partner didn't
invent the steamboat. They helped to make it practical.
Before railroads, rivers were the highways of the country.

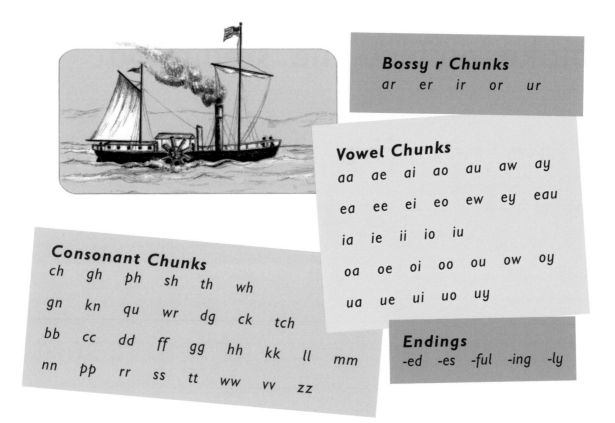

Bossy r Chunks

ar   er   ir   or   ur

Vowel Chunks

aa   ae   ai   ao   au   aw   ay

ea   ee   ei   eo   ew   ey   eau

ia   ie   ii   io   iu

oa   oe   oi   oo   ou   ow   oy

ua   ue   ui   uo   uy

Consonant Chunks

ch   gh   ph   sh   th   wh

gn   kn   qu   wr   dg   ck   tch

bb   cc   dd   ff   gg   hh   kk   ll   mm

nn   pp   rr   ss   tt   ww   vv   zz

Endings

-ed   -es   -ful   -ing   -ly

Copy and chunk the story.

The steamboat began to move

T

steadily up the Hudson River. It

s

cruised along, passing all the other

c

boats as though they were

b

standing still. Robert Fulton and

s

his partner didn't invent the

h

steamboat. They helped to make it

s

practical. Before railroads, rivers

P

were the highways of the country.

W

1. Read the story to your student.

2. Read it together slowly. Have the student look carefully at each word as you read.

3. Together, mark the <u>vowel chunks</u> (yellow), <u>consonant chunks</u> (blue), <u>**Bossy *r* chunks**</u> (purple), <u>**Tricky *y* Guy**</u> (green), <u>endings</u> (pink or red), and <u>silent letters</u> (orange).

Would it explode? Would it catch fire? Would it sink? Many people on the dock didn't think the new steamboat would go anywhere. The paddle wheel churned, and smoke puffed. The steamboat began to move steadily up the Hudson River. It cruised along, passing all the other boats as though they were standing still. Robert Fulton and his partner didn't invent the steamboat. They helped to make it practical. Before railroads, rivers were the highways of the country.

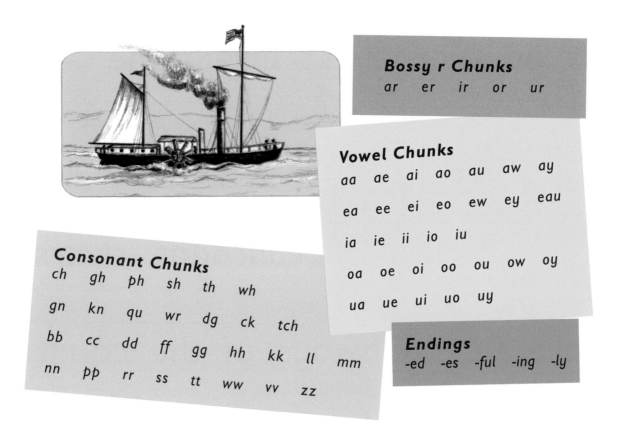

Bossy r Chunks

ar   er   ir   or   ur

Vowel Chunks

aa	ae	ai	ao	au	aw	ay
ea	ee	ei	eo	ew	ey	eau
ia	ie	ii	io	iu		
oa	oe	oi	oo	ou	ow	oy
ua	ue	ui	uo	uy		

Consonant Chunks

ch	gh	ph	sh	th	wh	
gn	kn	qu	wr	dg	ck	tch
bb	cc	dd	ff	gg	hh	kk	ll	mm
nn	pp	rr	ss	tt	ww	vv	zz

Endings

-ed   -es   -ful   -ing   -ly

Copy and chunk the story.

Would it explode? Would it catch

W

fire? Would it sink? Many people

f

on the dock didn't think the new

o

steamboat would go anywhere.

s

The paddle wheel churned, and

T

smoke puffed. The steamboat

s

began to move steadily up the

b

Hudson River.

H

1. Read the story to your student.

2. Read it together slowly. Have the student look carefully at each word as you read.

3. Together, mark the **vowel chunks** (yellow), **consonant chunks** (blue), **Bossy _r_ chunks** (purple), **Tricky _y_ Guy** (green), **endings** (pink or red), and **silent letters** (orange).

Would it explode? Would it catch fire? Would it sink? Many people on the dock didn't think the new steamboat would go anywhere. The paddle wheel churned, and smoke puffed. The steamboat began to move steadily up the Hudson River. It cruised along, passing all the other boats as though they were standing still. Robert Fulton and his partner didn't invent the steamboat. They helped to make it practical. Before railroads, rivers were the highways of the country.

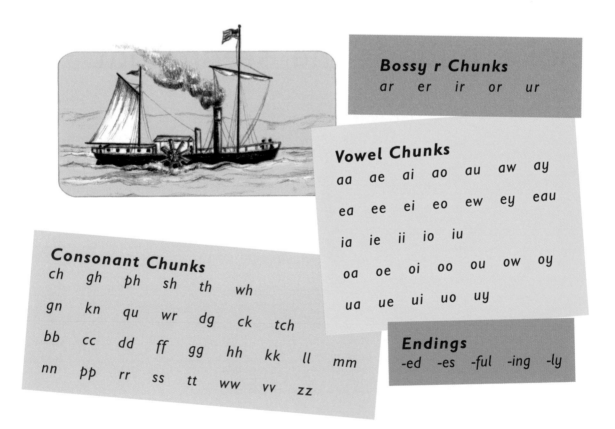

Bossy r Chunks

ar   er   ir   or   ur

Vowel Chunks

aa ae ai ao au aw ay

ea ee ei eo ew ey eau

ia ie ii io iu

oa oe oi oo ou ow oy

ua ue ui uo uy

Consonant Chunks

ch   gh   ph   sh   th   wh

gn   kn   qu   wr   dg   ck   tch

bb   cc   dd   ff   gg   hh   kk   ll   mm

nn   pp   rr   ss   tt   ww   vv   zz

Endings

-ed -es -ful -ing -ly

Write this week's story from dictation. Take your time and ask for help if you need it.

Would

I spelled _____ words correctly.

1. Read the story to your student.

2. Read it together slowly. Have the student look carefully at each word as you read.

3. Together, mark the **vowel chunks** (yellow), **consonant chunks** (blue), **Bossy _r_ chunks** (purple), **Tricky _y_ Guy** (green), **endings** (pink or red), and **silent letters** (orange).

Would it explode? Would it catch fire? Would it sink?
Many people on the dock didn't think the new steamboat
would go anywhere. The paddle wheel churned, and smoke
puffed. The steamboat began to move steadily up the Hudson
River. It cruised along, passing all the other boats as though
they were standing still. Robert Fulton and his partner didn't
invent the steamboat. They helped to make it practical.
Before railroads, rivers were the highways of the country.

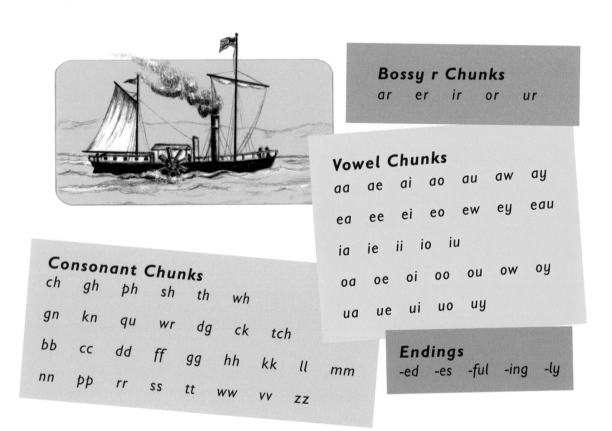

Bossy r Chunks

ar   er   ir   or   ur

Vowel Chunks

aa   ae   ai   ao   au   aw   ay

ea   ee   ei   eo   ew   ey   eau

ia   ie   ii   io   iu

oa   oe   oi   oo   ou   ow   oy

ua   ue   ui   uo   uy

Consonant Chunks

ch   gh   ph   sh   th   wh

gn   kn   qu   wr   dg   ck   tch

bb   cc   dd   ff   gg   hh   kk   ll   mm

nn   pp   rr   ss   tt   ww   vv   zz

Endings

-ed   -es   -ful   -ing   -ly

See if you can write this week's story from dictation without asking for help.

I spelled _____ words correctly.

1. Read the story to your student.

2. Read it together slowly. Have the student look carefully at each word as you read.

3. This week you and your student will be looking for and marking all six letter patterns that you have learned. They are **vowel chunks** (yellow), **consonant chunks** (blue), **Bossy _r_ chunks** (purple), **Tricky _y_ Guy** (green), **endings** (pink or red), and **silent letters** (orange).

When it was finished, the Erie Canal linked the Hudson River to Lake Erie. Now there was a safer and cheaper way to get from New York City to the Great Lakes. Some travelers enjoyed the slow, easy pace. They liked the view from the boat's top deck. But people had to listen for the warning, "Low bridge! Everybody down!" Otherwise, they might get knocked overboard!

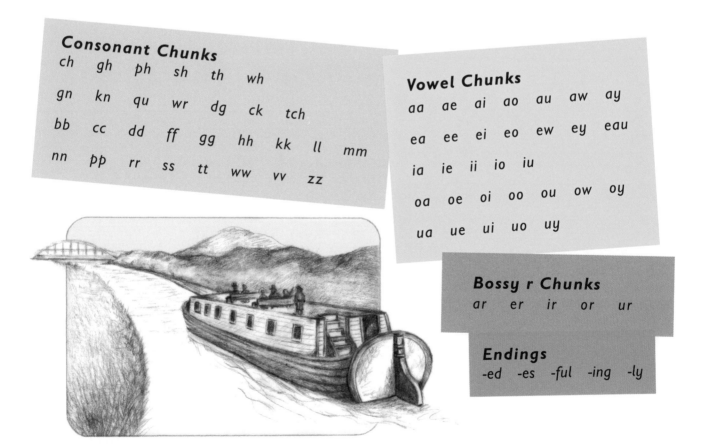

Consonant Chunks

ch   gh   ph   sh   th   wh

gn   kn   qu   wr   dg   ck   tch

bb   cc   dd   ff   gg   hh   kk   ll   mm

nn   pp   rr   ss   tt   ww   vv   zz

Vowel Chunks

aa   ae   ai   ao   au   aw   ay

ea   ee   ei   eo   ew   ey   eau

ia   ie   ii   io   iu

oa   oe   oi   oo   ou   ow   oy

ua   ue   ui   uo   uy

Bossy r Chunks

ar   er   ir   or   ur

Endings

-ed   -es   -ful   -ing   -ly

Copy and chunk the story.

When it was finished, the Erie

W

Canal linked the Hudson River to

C

Lake Erie. Now there was a safer

L

and cheaper way to get from

a

New York City to the Great Lakes.

N

Some travelers enjoyed the slow,

S

easy pace. They liked the view

e

from the boat's top deck.

f

1. Read the story to your student.

2. Read it together slowly. Have the student look carefully at each word as you read.

3. Together, mark the <u>**vowel chunks**</u> (yellow), <u>**consonant chunks**</u> (blue), <u>**Bossy r chunks**</u> (purple), <u>**Tricky y Guy**</u> (green), <u>**endings**</u> (pink or red), and <u>**silent letters**</u> (orange).

When it was finished, the Erie Canal linked the Hudson River to Lake Erie. Now there was a safer and cheaper way to get from New York City to the Great Lakes. Some travelers enjoyed the slow, easy pace. They liked the view from the boat's top deck. But people had to listen for the warning, "Low bridge! Everybody down!" Otherwise, they might get knocked overboard!

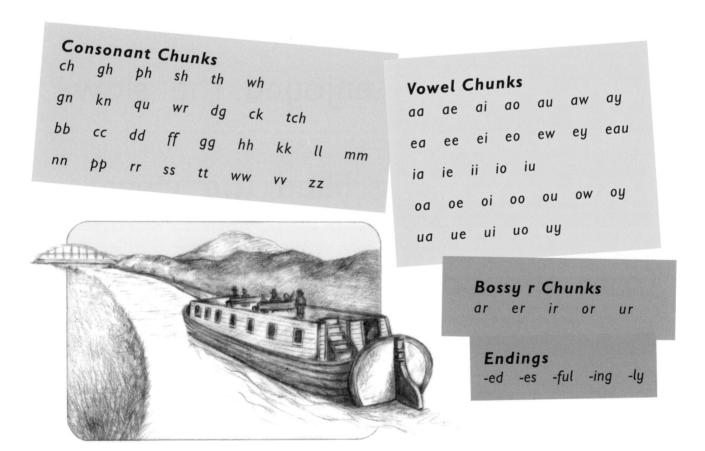

Consonant Chunks

ch gh ph sh th wh
gn kn qu wr dg ck tch
bb cc dd ff gg hh kk ll mm
nn pp rr ss tt ww vv zz

Vowel Chunks

aa ae ai ao au aw ay
ea ee ei eo ew ey eau
ia ie ii io iu
oa oe oi oo ou ow oy
ua ue ui uo uy

Bossy r Chunks
ar er ir or ur

Endings
-ed -es -ful -ing -ly

Section 2: Copywork

Copy and chunk the story.

Now there was a safer way to

N

get from New York City to the

g

Great Lakes. Some travelers

G

enjoyed the slow, easy pace. They

e

liked the view from the boat's

l

top deck. But people had to listen

t

for the warning, "Low bridge!

f

Everybody down!" Otherwise,

E

they might get knocked overboard!

t

1. Read the story to your student.

2. Read it together slowly. Have the student look carefully at each word as you read.

3. Together, mark the **vowel chunks** (yellow), **consonant chunks** (blue), **Bossy *r* chunks** (purple), **Tricky *y* Guy** (green), **endings** (pink or red), and **silent letters** (orange).

When it was finished, the Erie Canal linked the Hudson River to Lake Erie. Now there was a safer and cheaper way to get from New York City to the Great Lakes. Some travelers enjoyed the slow, easy pace. They liked the view from the boat's top deck. But people had to listen for the warning, "Low bridge! Everybody down!" Otherwise, they might get knocked overboard!

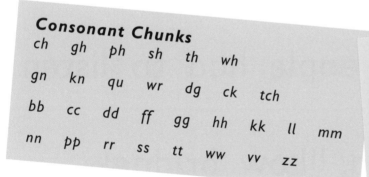

Consonant Chunks

ch   gh   ph   sh   th   wh
gn   kn   qu   wr   dg   ck   tch
bb   cc   dd   ff   gg   hh   kk   ll   mm
nn   pp   rr   ss   tt   ww   vv   zz

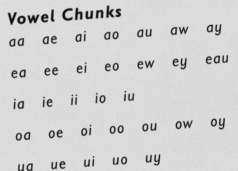

Vowel Chunks

aa   ae   ai   ao   au   aw   ay
ea   ee   ei   eo   ew   ey   eau
ia   ie   ii   io   iu
oa   oe   oi   oo   ou   ow   oy
ua   ue   ui   uo   uy

Bossy r Chunks
ar   er   ir   or   ur

Endings
-ed   -es   -ful   -ing   -ly

Copy and chunk the story.

When it was finished, the Erie

W

Canal linked the Hudson River to

C

Lake Erie. Now there was a safer

L

and cheaper way to get from

a

New York City to the Great Lakes.

N

Some travelers enjoyed the slow,

S

easy pace. They liked the view

e

from the boat's top deck.

f

1. Read the story to your student.

2. Read it together slowly. Have the student look carefully at each word as you read.

3. Together, mark the **vowel chunks** (yellow), **consonant chunks** (blue), **Bossy *r* chunks** (purple), **Tricky *y* Guy** (green), **endings** (pink or red), and **silent letters** (orange).

When it was finished, the Erie Canal linked the Hudson River to Lake Erie. Now there was a safer and cheaper way to get from New York City to the Great Lakes. Some travelers enjoyed the slow, easy pace. They liked the view from the boat's top deck. But people had to listen for the warning, "Low bridge! Everybody down!" Otherwise, they might get knocked overboard!

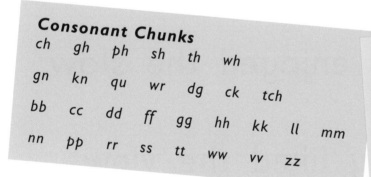

Consonant Chunks

ch gh ph sh th wh
gn kn qu wr dg ck tch
bb cc dd ff gg hh kk ll mm
nn pp rr ss tt ww vv zz

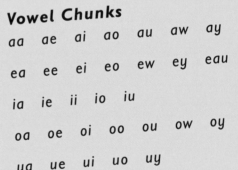

Vowel Chunks

aa ae ai ao au aw ay
ea ee ei eo ew ey eau
ia ie ii io iu
oa oe oi oo ou ow oy
ua ue ui uo uy

Bossy r Chunks

ar er ir or ur

Endings

-ed -es -ful -ing -ly

Section 2: First Dictation

Write this week's story from dictation. Take your time and ask for help if you need it.

When

1. Read the story to your student.

2. Read it together slowly. Have the student look carefully at each word as you read.

3. Together, mark the <u>**vowel chunks**</u> (yellow), <u>**consonant chunks**</u> (blue), <u>**Bossy *r* chunks**</u> (purple), <u>**Tricky *y* Guy**</u> (green), <u>**endings**</u> (pink or red), and <u>**silent letters**</u> (orange).

When it was finished, the Erie Canal linked the Hudson River to Lake Erie. Now there was a safer and cheaper way to get from New York City to the Great Lakes. Some travelers enjoyed the slow, easy pace. They liked the view from the boat's top deck. But people had to listen for the warning, "Low bridge! Everybody down!" Otherwise, they might get knocked overboard!

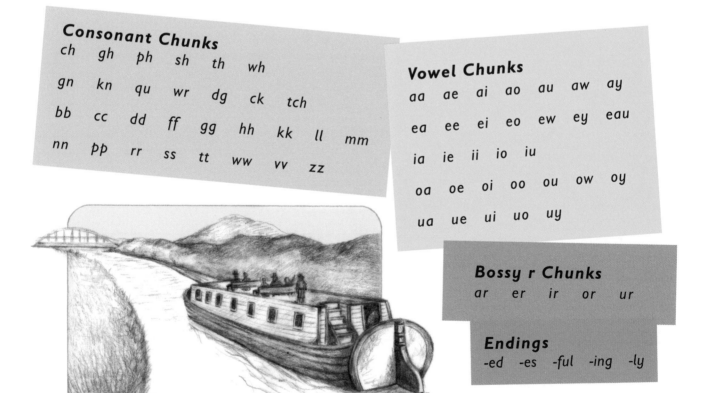

Consonant Chunks

ch   gh   ph   sh   th   wh

gn   kn   qu   wr   dg   ck   tch

bb   cc   dd   ff   gg   hh   kk   ll   mm

nn   pp   rr   ss   tt   ww   vv   zz

Vowel Chunks

aa   ae   ai   ao   au   aw   ay

ea   ee   ei   eo   ew   ey   eau

ia   ie   ii   io   iu

oa   oe   oi   oo   ou   ow   oy

ua   ue   ui   uo   uy

Bossy r Chunks

ar   er   ir   or   ur

Endings

-ed   -es   -ful   -ing   -ly

Section 2: Second Dictation

See if you can write this week's story from dictation without asking for help.

I spelled _____ words correctly.

1. Read the story to your student.

2. Read it together slowly. Have the student look carefully at each word as you read.

3. This week you and your student will be looking for and marking all six letter patterns that you have learned. They are **vowel chunks** (yellow), **consonant chunks** (blue), **Bossy *r* chunks** (purple), **Tricky *y* Guy** (green), **endings** (pink or red), and **silent letters** (orange).

"Step right up! Step right up! The show is about to begin!" Circuses used to perform in special buildings in big cities. In 1825 one American circus used a large canvas tent for the first time. What a great idea! Now a circus could be held in any city or town. The circus traveled in wagons from place to place. Later, P. T. Barnum began using special train cars to move the circus even farther and faster.

Endings
-ed   -es   -ful   -ing   -ly

Bossy r Chunks
ar   er   ir   or   ur

Vowel Chunks
aa   ae   ai   ao   au   aw   ay
ea   ee   ei   eo   ew   ey   eau
ia   ie   ii   io   iu
oa   oe   oi   oo   ou   ow   oy
ua   ue   ui   uo   uy

Consonant Chunks
ch   gh   ph   sh   th   wh
gn   kn   qu   wr   dg   ck   tch
bb   cc   dd   ff   gg   hh   kk   ll   mm
nn   pp   rr   ss   tt   ww   vv   zz

Copy and chunk the story.

"Step right up! Step right up!

"S

The show is about to begin!"

T

Circuses used to perform in

C

special buildings in big cities. In

s

1825 one American circus used

1

a large canvas tent for the first

a

time. What a great idea! Now a

t

circus could be held in any city

c

or town.

o

1. Read the story to your student.

2. Read it together slowly. Have the student look carefully at each word as you read.

3. Together, mark the **vowel chunks** (yellow), **consonant chunks** (blue), **Bossy _r_ chunks** (purple), **Tricky _y_ Guy** (green), **endings** (pink or red), and **silent letters** (orange).

"Step right up! Step right up! The show is about to begin!" Circuses used to perform in special buildings in big cities. In 1825 one American circus used a large canvas tent for the first time. What a great idea! Now a circus could be held in any city or town. The circus traveled in wagons from place to place. Later, P. T. Barnum began using special train cars to move the circus even farther and faster.

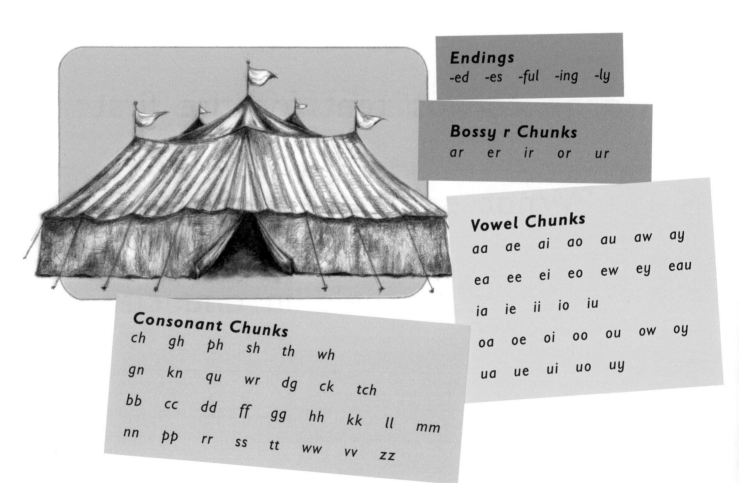

Endings
-ed -es -ful -ing -ly

Bossy r Chunks
ar er ir or ur

Vowel Chunks
aa ae ai ao au aw ay
ea ee ei eo ew ey eau
ia ie ii io iu
oa oe oi oo ou ow oy
ua ue ui uo uy

Consonant Chunks
ch gh ph sh th wh
gn kn qu wr dg ck tch
bb cc dd ff gg hh kk ll mm
nn pp rr ss tt ww vv zz

Copy and chunk the story.

In 1825 one American circus used

a large canvas tent for the first

time. What a great idea! Now a

circus could be held in any city or

town. The circus traveled in

wagons from place to place. Later,

P. T. Barnum began using special

train cars to move the circus even

farther and faster.

1. Read the story to your student.

2. Read it together slowly. Have the student look carefully at each word as you read.

3. Together, mark the **vowel chunks** (yellow), **consonant chunks** (blue), **Bossy _r_ chunks** (purple), **Tricky _y_ Guy** (green), **endings** (pink or red), and **silent letters** (orange).

"Step right up! Step right up! The show is about to begin!"
Circuses used to perform in special buildings in big cities.
In 1825 one American circus used a large canvas tent for the
first time. What a great idea! Now a circus could be held in
any city or town. The circus traveled in wagons from place
to place. Later, P. T. Barnum began using special train cars to
move the circus even farther and faster.

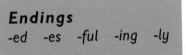

Endings
-ed   -es   -ful   -ing   -ly

Bossy r Chunks
ar   er   ir   or   ur

Vowel Chunks
aa   ae   ai   ao   au   aw   ay
ea   ee   ei   eo   ew   ey   eau
ia   ie   ii   io   iu
oa   oe   oi   oo   ou   ow   oy
ua   ue   ui   uo   uy

Consonant Chunks
ch   gh   ph   sh   th   wh
gn   kn   qu   wr   dg   ck   tch
bb   cc   dd   ff   gg   hh   kk   ll   mm
nn   pp   rr   ss   tt   ww   vv   zz

Section 2: Copywork

Copy and chunk the story.

"Step right up! Step right up!

"S

The show is about to begin!"

T

Circuses used to perform in

C

special buildings in big cities. In

s

1825 one American circus used

1

a large canvas tent for the first

a

time. What a great idea! Now a

t

circus could be held in any city

c

or town.

o

1. Read the story to your student.

2. Read it together slowly. Have the student look carefully at each word as you read.

3. Together, mark the **vowel chunks** (yellow), **consonant chunks** (blue), **Bossy *r* chunks** (purple), **Tricky *y* Guy** (green), **endings** (pink or red), and **silent letters** (orange).

"Step right up! Step right up! The show is about to begin!" Circuses used to perform in special buildings in big cities. In **1825** one American circus used a large canvas tent for the first time. What a great idea! Now a circus could be held in any city or town. The circus traveled in wagons from place to place. Later, P. T. Barnum began using special train cars to move the circus even farther and faster.

Endings
-ed   -es   -ful   -ing   -ly

Bossy r Chunks
ar   er   ir   or   ur

Vowel Chunks
aa   ae   ai   ao   au   aw   ay
ea   ee   ei   eo   ew   ey   eau
ia   ie   ii   io   iu
oa   oe   oi   oo   ou   ow   oy
ua   ue   ui   uo   uy

Consonant Chunks
ch   gh   ph   sh   th   wh
gn   kn   qu   wr   dg   ck   tch
bb   cc   dd   ff   gg   hh   kk   ll   mm
nn   pp   rr   ss   tt   ww   vv   zz

Section 2: First Dictation

Write this week's story from dictation. Take your time and ask for help if you need it.

"Step

I spelled _____ words correctly.   **151**

1. Read the story to your student.

2. Read it together slowly. Have the student look carefully at each word as you read.

3. Together, mark the <u>vowel chunks</u> (yellow), <u>consonant chunks</u> (blue), <u>Bossy *r* chunks</u> (purple), <u>Tricky *y* Guy</u> (green), <u>endings</u> (pink or red), and <u>silent letters</u> (orange).

"Step right up! Step right up! The show is about to begin!" Circuses used to perform in special buildings in big cities. In 1825 one American circus used a large canvas tent for the first time. What a great idea! Now a circus could be held in any city or town. The circus traveled in wagons from place to place. Later, P. T. Barnum began using special train cars to move the circus even farther and faster.

Endings
-ed   -es   -ful   -ing   -ly

Bossy r Chunks
ar   er   ir   or   ur

Vowel Chunks
aa   ae   ai   ao   au   aw   ay
ea   ee   ei   eo   ew   ey   eau
ia   ie   ii   io   iu
oa   oe   oi   oo   ou   ow   oy
ua   ue   ui   uo   uy

Consonant Chunks
ch   gh   ph   sh   th   wh
gn   kn   qu   wr   dg   ck   tch
bb   cc   dd   ff   gg   hh   kk   ll   mm
nn   pp   rr   ss   tt   ww   vv   zz

Section 2: Second Dictation

See if you can write this week's story from dictation without asking for help.

I spelled _____ words correctly.

1. Read the story to your student.

2. Read it together slowly. Have the student look carefully at each word as you read.

3. This week you and your student will be looking for and marking all six letter patterns that you have learned. They are <u>vowel chunks</u> (yellow), <u>consonant chunks</u> (blue), <u>**Bossy r chunks**</u> (purple), <u>**Tricky y Guy**</u> (green), <u>endings</u> (pink or red), and <u>silent letters</u> (orange).

How could anyone own a person? How could some states allow slavery? Harriet Beecher Stowe believed that slavery was wrong. She knew she had to do something. She wrote stories told from a slave's point of view. The stories became a book called *Uncle Tom's Cabin.* Harriet made the everyday life of slaves real to others. Many people read her book and talked about it. Her writing made a difference.

Consonant Chunks

ch   gh   ph   sh   th   wh

gn   kn   qu   wr   dg   ck   tch

bb   cc   dd   ff   gg   hh   kk   ll   mm

nn   pp   rr   ss   tt   ww   vv   zz

Vowel Chunks

aa   ae   ai   ao   au   aw   ay

ea   ee   ei   eo   ew   ey   eau

ia   ie   ii   io   iu

oa   oe   oi   oo   ou   ow   oy

ua   ue   ui   uo   uy

Endings

-ed   -es   -ful   -ing   -ly

Bossy r Chunks

ar   er   ir   or   ur

Copy and chunk the story.

How could anyone own a person?

H

How could some states allow

H

slavery? Harriet Beecher Stowe

s

believed that slavery was wrong.

b

She knew she had to do

S

something. She wrote stories told

s

from a slave's point of view. The

f

stories became a book called

s

Uncle Tom's Cabin.

U

16B

1. Read the story to your student.

2. Read it together slowly. Have the student look carefully at each word as you read.

3. Together, mark the **vowel chunks** (yellow), **consonant chunks** (blue), **Bossy _r_ chunks** (purple), **Tricky _y_ Guy** (green), **endings** (pink or red), and **silent letters** (orange).

How could anyone own a person? How could some states allow slavery? Harriet Beecher Stowe believed that slavery was wrong. She knew she had to do something. She wrote stories told from a slave's point of view. The stories became a book called _Uncle Tom's Cabin._ Harriet made the everyday life of slaves real to others. Many people read her book and talked about it. Her writing made a difference.

Consonant Chunks

ch	gh	ph	sh	th	wh		
gn	kn	qu	wr	dg	ck	tch	
bb	cc	dd	ff	gg	hh	kk	ll	mm
nn	pp	rr	ss	tt	ww	vv	zz

Vowel Chunks

aa	ae	ai	ao	au	aw	ay
ea	ee	ei	eo	ew	ey	eau
ia	ie	ii	io	iu		
oa	oe	oi	oo	ou	ow	oy
ua	ue	ui	uo	uy		

Endings
-ed -es -ful -ing -ly

Bossy r Chunks
ar er ir or ur

Copy and chunk the story.

She knew she had to do

S

something. She wrote stories told

s

from a slave's point of view. The

f

stories became a book called

s

<u>Uncle Tom's Cabin</u>. Harriet made

U

the everyday life of slaves real

t

to others. Many people read her

t

book and talked about it. Her

b

writing made a difference.

W

1. Read the story to your student.

2. Read it together slowly. Have the student look carefully at each word as you read.

3. Together, mark the **vowel chunks** (yellow), **consonant chunks** (blue), **Bossy *r* chunks** (purple), **Tricky *y* Guy** (green), **endings** (pink or red), and **silent letters** (orange).

How could anyone own a person? How could some states allow slavery? Harriet Beecher Stowe believed that slavery was wrong. She knew she had to do something. She wrote stories told from a slave's point of view. The stories became a book called *Uncle Tom's Cabin*. Harriet made the everyday life of slaves real to others. Many people read her book and talked about it. Her writing made a difference.

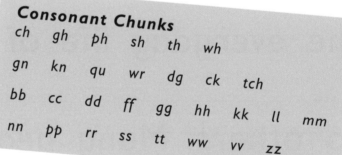

Consonant Chunks

ch	gh	ph	sh	th	wh			
gn	kn	qu	wr	dg	ck	tch		
bb	cc	dd	ff	gg	hh	kk	ll	mm
nn	pp	rr	ss	tt	ww	vv	zz	

Vowel Chunks

aa	ae	ai	ao	au	aw	ay
ea	ee	ei	eo	ew	ey	eau
ia	ie	ii	io	iu		
oa	oe	oi	oo	ou	ow	oy
ua	ue	ui	uo	uy		

Endings

-ed   -es   -ful   -ing   -ly

Bossy r Chunks

ar   er   ir   or   ur

Copy and chunk the story.

How could anyone own a person?

H

How could some states allow

H

slavery? Harriet Beecher Stowe

s

believed that slavery was wrong.

b

She knew she had to do

S

something. She wrote stories told

s

from a slave's point of view. The

f

stories became a book called

s

Uncle Tom's Cabin.

U

1. Read the story to your student.

2. Read it together slowly. Have the student look carefully at each word as you read.

3. Together, mark the **vowel chunks** (yellow), **consonant chunks** (blue), **Bossy *r* chunks** (purple), **Tricky *y* Guy** (green), **endings** (pink or red), and **silent letters** (orange).

How could anyone own a person? How could some states allow slavery? Harriet Beecher Stowe believed that slavery was wrong. She knew she had to do something. She wrote stories told from a slave's point of view. The stories became a book called *Uncle Tom's Cabin*. Harriet made the everyday life of slaves real to others. Many people read her book and talked about it. Her writing made a difference.

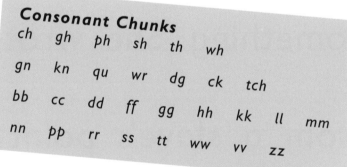

Consonant Chunks

ch   gh   ph   sh   th   wh
gn   kn   qu   wr   dg   ck   tch
bb   cc   dd   ff   gg   hh   kk   ll   mm
nn   pp   rr   ss   tt   ww   vv   zz

Vowel Chunks

aa   ae   ai   ao   au   aw   ay
ea   ee   ei   eo   ew   ey   eau
ia   ie   ii   io   iu
oa   oe   oi   oo   ou   ow   oy
ua   ue   ui   uo   uy

Endings

-ed   -es   -ful   -ing   -ly

Bossy r Chunks

ar   er   ir   or   ur

Write this week's story from dictation. Take your time and ask for help if you need it.

How

1. Read the story to your student.

2. Read it together slowly. Have the student look carefully at each word as you read.

3. Together, mark the **vowel chunks** (yellow), **consonant chunks** (blue), **Bossy _r_ chunks** (purple), **Tricky _y_ Guy** (green), **endings** (pink or red), and **silent letters** (orange).

How could anyone own a person? How could some states allow slavery? Harriet Beecher Stowe believed that slavery was wrong. She knew she had to do something. She wrote stories told from a slave's point of view. The stories became a book called _Uncle Tom's Cabin_. Harriet made the everyday life of slaves real to others. Many people read her book and talked about it. Her writing made a difference.

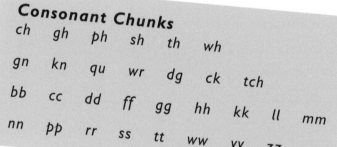

Consonant Chunks

ch gh ph sh th wh
gn kn qu wr dg ck tch
bb cc dd ff gg hh kk ll mm
nn pp rr ss tt ww vv zz

Vowel Chunks

aa ae ai ao au aw ay
ea ee ei eo ew ey eau
ia ie ii io iu
oa oe oi oo ou ow oy
ua ue ui uo uy

Endings
-ed -es -ful -ing -ly

Bossy r Chunks
ar er ir or ur

Section 2: Second Dictation

See if you can write this week's story from dictation without asking for help.

I spelled _____ words correctly.

1. Read the story to your student.

2. Read it together slowly. Have the student look carefully at each word as you read.

3. Together, mark the <u>**vowel chunks**</u>, <u>**consonant chunks**</u>, <u>**Bossy *r* chunks**</u>, <u>**Tricky *y* Guy**</u>, <u>**endings**</u>, and <u>**silent letters**</u>, using the correct colors for each.

Alexander Graham Bell was interested in hearing and speech. His mother was deaf. His wife was deaf, too. He did experiments. He taught many students how to speak more clearly. He also enjoyed inventing. Aleck built a machine that could send sounds over wires. The telephone changed how people lived. Now they could easily talk to anyone else who had a phone.

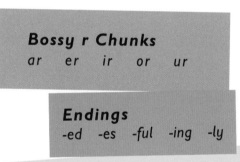

Bossy r Chunks
ar   er   ir   or   ur

Endings
-ed   -es   -ful   -ing   -ly

Vowel Chunks
aa   ae   ai   ao   au   aw   ay
ea   ee   ei   eo   ew   ey   eau
ia   ie   ii   io   iu
oa   oe   oi   oo   ou   ow   oy
ua   ue   ui   uo   uy

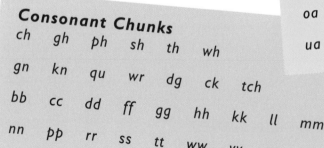

Consonant Chunks
ch   gh   ph   sh   th   wh
gn   kn   qu   wr   dg   ck   tch
bb   cc   dd   ff   gg   hh   kk   ll   mm
nn   pp   rr   ss   tt   ww   vv   zz

Copy and chunk the story.

Alexander Graham Bell was

A

interested in hearing and speech.

i

His mother was deaf. His wife

H

was deaf, too. He did experiments.

w

He taught many students how to

H

speak more clearly. He also

s

enjoyed inventing. Aleck built a

e

machine that could send sounds

m

over wires.

o

1. Read the story to your student.

2. Read it together slowly. Have the student look carefully at each word as you read.

3. Together, mark the <u>vowel chunks</u>, <u>consonant chunks</u>, <u>Bossy *r* chunks</u>, <u>Tricky *y* Guy</u>, <u>endings</u>, and <u>silent letters</u>, using the correct colors for each.

Alexander Graham Bell was interested in hearing and speech. His mother was deaf. His wife was deaf, too. He did experiments. He taught many students how to speak more clearly. He also enjoyed inventing. Aleck built a machine that could send sounds over wires. The telephone changed how people lived. Now they could easily talk to anyone else who had a phone.

Bossy r Chunks
ar   er   ir   or   ur

Endings
-ed   -es   -ful   -ing   -ly

Vowel Chunks
aa   ae   ai   ao   au   aw   ay
ea   ee   ei   eo   ew   ey   eau
ia   ie   ii   io   iu
oa   oe   oi   oo   ou   ow   oy
ua   ue   ui   uo   uy

Consonant Chunks
ch   gh   ph   sh   th   wh
gn   kn   qu   wr   dg   ck   tch
bb   cc   dd   ff   gg   hh   kk   ll   mm
nn   pp   rr   ss   tt   ww   vv   zz

Copy and chunk the story.

His wife was deaf, too. He did

H

experiments. He taught many

e

students how to speak more

s

clearly. He also enjoyed inventing.

c

Aleck built a machine that could

A

send sounds over wires. The

s

telephone changed how people

t

lived. Now they could easily talk

l

to anyone else who had a phone.

t

1. Read the story to your student.

2. Read it together slowly. Have the student look carefully at each word as you read.

3. Together, mark the **vowel chunks**, **consonant chunks**, **Bossy _r_ chunks**, **Tricky _y_ Guy**, **endings**, and **silent letters**, using the correct colors for each.

Alexander Graham Bell was interested in hearing and speech. His mother was deaf. His wife was deaf, too. He did experiments. He taught many students how to speak more clearly. He also enjoyed inventing. Aleck built a machine that could send sounds over wires. The telephone changed how people lived. Now they could easily talk to anyone else who had a phone.

Bossy r Chunks

ar   er   ir   or   ur

Endings

-ed   -es   -ful   -ing   -ly

Vowel Chunks

aa   ae   ai   ao   au   aw   ay

ea   ee   ei   eo   ew   ey   eau

ia   ie   ii   io   iu

oa   oe   oi   oo   ou   ow   oy

ua   ue   ui   uo   uy

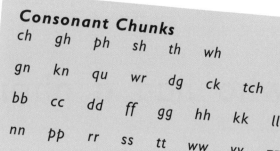

Consonant Chunks

ch   gh   ph   sh   th   wh

gn   kn   qu   wr   dg   ck   tch

bb   cc   dd   ff   gg   hh   kk   ll   mm

nn   pp   rr   ss   tt   ww   vv   zz

Copy and chunk the story.

Alexander Graham Bell was

A

interested in hearing and speech.

i

His mother was deaf. His wife

H

was deaf, too. He did experiments.

w

He taught many students how to

H

speak more clearly. He also

s

enjoyed inventing. Aleck built a

e

machine that could send sounds

m

over wires.

o

17D

Section 1: All Letter Patterns

1. Read the story to your student.

2. Read it together slowly. Have the student look carefully at each word as you read.

3. Together, mark the **vowel chunks**, **consonant chunks**, **Bossy r chunks**, **Tricky _y_ Guy**, **endings**, and **silent letters**, using the correct colors for each.

Alexander Graham Bell was interested in hearing and speech. His mother was deaf. His wife was deaf, too. He did experiments. He taught many students how to speak more clearly. He also enjoyed inventing. Aleck built a machine that could send sounds over wires. The telephone changed how people lived. Now they could easily talk to anyone else who had a phone.

Bossy r Chunks
ar er ir or ur

Endings
-ed -es -ful -ing -ly

Vowel Chunks
aa ae ai ao au aw ay
ea ee ei eo ew ey eau
ia ie ii io iu
oa oe oi oo ou ow oy
ua ue ui uo uy

Consonant Chunks
ch gh ph sh th wh
gn kn qu wr dg ck tch
bb cc dd ff gg hh kk ll mm
nn pp rr ss tt ww vv zz

Section 2: First Dictation

Write this week's story from dictation. Take your time and ask for help if you need it.

Alexander

1. Read the story to your student.

2. Read it together slowly. Have the student look carefully at each word as you read.

3. Together, mark the <u>vowel chunks</u>, <u>consonant chunks</u>, <u>Bossy *r* chunks</u>, <u>Tricky *y* Guy</u>, <u>endings</u>, and <u>silent letters</u>, using the correct colors for each.

Alexander Graham Bell was interested in hearing and speech. His mother was deaf. His wife was deaf, too. He did experiments. He taught many students how to speak more clearly. He also enjoyed inventing. Aleck built a machine that could send sounds over wires. The telephone changed how people lived. Now they could easily talk to anyone else who had a phone.

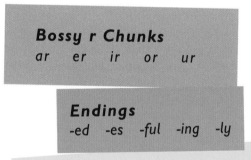

Bossy r Chunks

ar   er   ir   or   ur

Endings

-ed   -es   -ful   -ing   -ly

Vowel Chunks

aa   ae   ai   ao   au   aw   ay

ea   ee   ei   eo   ew   ey   eau

ia   ie   ii   io   iu

oa   oe   oi   oo   ou   ow   oy

ua   ue   ui   uo   uy

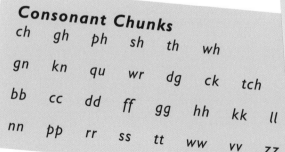

Consonant Chunks

ch   gh   ph   sh   th   wh

gn   kn   qu   wr   dg   ck   tch

bb   cc   dd   ff   gg   hh   kk   ll   mm

nn   pp   rr   ss   tt   ww   vv   zz

Section 2: Second Dictation

See if you can write this week's story from dictation without asking for help.

I spelled _____ words correctly.

1. Read the story to your student.

2. Read it together slowly. Have the student look carefully at each word as you read.

3. Together, mark the **vowel chunks**, **consonant chunks**, **Bossy _r_ chunks**, **Tricky _y_ Guy**, **endings**, and <u>silent letters</u>, using the correct colors for each.

Tom was always curious. What makes this work? Could it be improved? He tinkered. He learned. Sometimes he failed. But he kept trying and working hard. One of his ideas was an electric light bulb that would keep working for a long time. It was a success! Thomas Edison gathered a group of scientists to work together on new inventions. Today we call this place a research lab. By the time Tom died, his group had over 1,000 patents.

Vowel Chunks

aa ae ai ao au aw ay

ea ee ei eo ew ey eau

ia ie ii io iu

oa oe oi oo ou ow oy

ua ue ui uo uy

Endings
-ed -es -ful -ing -ly

Bossy r Chunks
ar er ir or ur

Consonant Chunks

ch gh ph sh th wh

gn kn qu wr dg ck tch

bb cc dd ff gg hh kk ll mm

nn pp rr ss tt ww vv zz

Copy and chunk the story.

Tom was always curious. What

T

makes this work? Could it be

m

improved? He tinkered. He learned.

i

Sometimes he failed. But he kept

S

trying and working hard. One of

t

his ideas was an electric light

h

bulb that would keep working for

b

a long time. It was a success!

a

1. Read the story to your student.

2. Read it together slowly. Have the student look carefully at each word as you read.

3. Together, mark the <u>**vowel chunks**</u>, <u>**consonant chunks**</u>, <u>**Bossy *r* chunks**</u>, <u>**Tricky *y* Guy**</u>, <u>**endings**</u>, and <u>**silent letters**</u>, using the correct colors for each.

Tom was always curious. What makes this work? Could it be improved? He tinkered. He learned. Sometimes he failed. But he kept trying and working hard. One of his ideas was an electric light bulb that would keep working for a long time. It was a success! Thomas Edison gathered a group of scientists to work together on new inventions. Today we call this place a research lab. By the time Tom died, his group had over 1,000 patents.

Vowel Chunks

aa ae ai ao au aw ay

ea ee ei eo ew ey eau

ia ie ii io iu

oa oe oi oo ou ow oy

ua ue ui uo uy

Endings
-ed -es -ful -ing -ly

Bossy r Chunks
ar er ir or ur

Consonant Chunks

ch gh ph sh th wh

gn kn qu wr dg ck tch

bb cc dd ff gg hh kk ll mm

nn pp rr ss tt ww vv zz

Copy and chunk the story.

One of his ideas was an electric

o

light bulb that would keep working

l

for a long time. It was a success!

f

Thomas Edison gathered a group

T

# of scientists to work together on

o

new inventions. Today we call this

n

place a research lab. By the time

P

Tom died, his group had over

T

1,000 patents.

1

18C

1. Read the story to your student.

2. Read it together slowly. Have the student look carefully at each word as you read.

3. Together, mark the <u>vowel chunks</u>, <u>consonant chunks</u>, <u>Bossy *r* chunks</u>, <u>Tricky *y* Guy</u>, <u>endings</u>, and <u>silent letters</u>, using the correct colors for each.

Tom was always curious. What makes this work? Could it be improved? He tinkered. He learned. Sometimes he failed. But he kept trying and working hard. One of his ideas was an electric light bulb that would keep working for a long time. It was a success! Thomas Edison gathered a group of scientists to work together on new inventions. Today we call this place a research lab. By the time Tom died, his group had over 1,000 patents.

Vowel Chunks

aa ae ai ao au aw ay

ea ee ei eo ew ey eau

ia ie ii io iu

oa oe oi oo ou ow oy

ua ue ui uo uy

Endings

-ed -es -ful -ing -ly

Bossy r Chunks

ar er ir or ur

Consonant Chunks

ch gh ph sh th wh

gn kn qu wr dg ck tch

bb cc dd ff gg hh kk ll mm

nn pp rr ss tt ww vv zz

Copy and chunk the story.

Tom was always curious. What

T

makes this work? Could it be

m

improved? He tinkered. He learned.

i

Sometimes he failed. But he kept

S

trying and working hard. One of

t

his ideas was an electric light

h

bulb that would keep working for

b

a long time. It was a success!

a

1. Read the story to your student.

2. Read it together slowly. Have the student look carefully at each word as you read.

3. Together, mark the **vowel chunks**, **consonant chunks**, **Bossy _r_ chunks**, **Tricky _y_ Guy**, **endings**, and **silent letters**, using the correct colors for each.

Tom was always curious. What makes this work? Could it be improved? He tinkered. He learned. Sometimes he failed. But he kept trying and working hard. One of his ideas was an electric light bulb that would keep working for a long time. It was a success! Thomas Edison gathered a group of scientists to work together on new inventions. Today we call this place a research lab. By the time Tom died, his group had over 1,000 patents.

Vowel Chunks

aa ae ai ao au aw ay

ea ee ei eo ew ey eau

ia ie ii io iu

oa oe oi oo ou ow oy

ua ue ui uo uy

Endings

-ed -es -ful -ing -ly

Bossy r Chunks

ar er ir or ur

Consonant Chunks

ch gh ph sh th wh

gn kn qu wr dg ck tch

bb cc dd ff gg hh kk ll mm

nn pp rr ss tt ww vv zz

Write this week's story from dictation. Take your time and ask for help if you need it.

Tom

I spelled _____ words correctly.

1. Read the story to your student.

2. Read it together slowly. Have the student look carefully at each word as you read.

3. Together, mark the <u>**vowel chunks**</u>, <u>**consonant chunks**</u>, <u>**Bossy *r* chunks**</u>, <u>**Tricky *y* Guy**</u>, <u>**endings**</u>, and <u>**silent letters**</u>, using the correct colors for each.

Tom was always curious. What makes this work? Could it be improved? He tinkered. He learned. Sometimes he failed. But he kept trying and working hard. One of his ideas was an electric light bulb that would keep working for a long time. It was a success! Thomas Edison gathered a group of scientists to work together on new inventions. Today we call this place a research lab. By the time Tom died, his group had over 1,000 patents.

Vowel Chunks
aa ae ai ao au aw ay
ea ee ei eo ew ey eau
ia ie ii io iu
oa oe oi oo ou ow oy
ua ue ui uo uy

Endings
-ed -es -ful -ing -ly

Bossy r Chunks
ar er ir or ur

Consonant Chunks
ch gh ph sh th wh
gn kn qu wr dg ck tch
bb cc dd ff gg hh kk ll mm
nn pp rr ss tt ww vv zz

Section 2: Second Dictation

See if you can write this week's story from dictation without asking for help.

I spelled _____ words correctly.